BRIGHT NOTES

MOBY DICK
BY
HERMAN MELVILLE

Intelligent Education

Nashville, Tennessee

BRIGHT NOTES: Moby Dick
www.BrightNotes.com

No part of this publication may be used or reproduced in any manner whatsoever without written permission, except in the case of brief quotations in critical articles and reviews. For permissions, contact Influence Publishers http://www.influencepublishers.com.

ISBN: 978-1-645422-08-2 (Paperback)
ISBN: 978-1-645422-09-9 (eBook)

Published in accordance with the U.S. Copyright Office Orphan Works and Mass Digitization report of the register of copyrights, June 2015.

Originally published by Monarch Press.
Laurence MacPhee; Elaine Pruitt, 1964
2019 Edition published by Influence Publishers.

Interior design by Lapiz Digital Services. Cover Design by Thinkpen Designs.

Printed in the United States of America.

Library of Congress Cataloging-in-Publication Data forthcoming.
Names: Intelligent Education
Title: BRIGHT NOTES: Moby Dick
Subject: STU004000 STUDY AIDS / Book Notes

CONTENTS

1) Introduction to Herman Melville — 1

2) Brief Summary of Moby Dick — 5

3) Textual Analysis
   - Chapters 1–9 — 10
   - Chapters 10–29 — 26
   - Chapters 30–45 — 44
   - Chapters 46–63 — 61
   - Chapters 64–81 — 78
   - Chapters 82–101 — 94
   - Chapters 102–118 — 115
   - Chapters 119–135 — 130

4) Character Analyses — 148

5) Critical Commentary — 157

6) Essay Questions and Answers — 162

7) Bibliography and Guide to Further Research — 169

INTRODUCTION TO HERMAN MELVILLE

MELVILLE'S LIFE

(1819–1891) Born into a family of substantial means in New York City on August 19, 1819, Herman Melville spent a secure and comfortable childhood. His maternal grandfather, Peter Gansevoort, had served as a general in the American Revolution, and his father, Allan Melvill (his father's spelling for the family name) was a successful importer. In 1830, however, his father suffered heavy financial reverses which were followed by serious illness culminating in his death in 1832.

Shocked by the death of his father whom he idolized, Melville moved with his family to Albany where he attended the Albany Classical School for a time. Here, constant friction with his mother, and his own restlessness soon brought an end to his spotty education, supplemented only by his avid reading of the books from his father's library.

Melville soon drifted into a variety of occupations. He worked for a time as a clerk in a store owned by an older brother, as a messenger for a bank, and later, as a country schoolteacher near his uncle's home in Pittsfield, Massachusetts. Finally in 1839, he signed on a British merchant ship, the St. Lawrence, bound to Liverpool and back, a trip which provided the material for his novel, *Redburn* (1849), and the impetus for an extended period of travel and adventure. Although he again tried school teaching on his return from Liverpool, he signed aboard the whaler Acushnet as an ordinary seaman in 1841.

After a trip around Cape Horn, Melville suffered the hardship of life aboard a mid-nineteenth century whaler until he could no longer tolerate it. Accordingly, he and a shipmate Tobias Greene (who appears as Toby in *Typee*) deserted the St. Lawrence at Nukuheva in the Marquesas Islands. Here Merville spent a month as the captive of a cannibal tribe, and finally escaped aboard the Australian whaler the Lucy Ann, which he left a short time later at Tahiti. Again after a short stay working at a variety of occupations, he signed aboard the whaler Charles and Henry, and arrived in Hawaii in April, 1843. Here, after working for a short time as a warehouse clerk, by now homesick for America, he joined the U.S. Navy and was assigned to the frigate United States. Fourteen months later, after visits to Mexico and South America, he was finally discharged in New York City in October, 1844, and with the exception of a few trips later in his life, he closed forever the period of his adventures.

In the years immediately following his travels, Melville began his career as a writer. In 1846 he published *Typee*, a somewhat exaggerated and imaginative account of his stay among the Typee islanders, and in 1847, its sequel *Omoo*. These were followed by *Mardi*, in 1849, an allegorical novel quite different from its predecessors and the precursor of *Moby Dick*. Attempting to atone for the failure of *Mardi*, Melville returned to the method of his earlier adventure books with *Redburn* (1849), which borrowed material from his first voyage to Liverpool in 1839; and *White Jacket* (1850), which enlarged upon his experience as a seaman aboard the United States.

Although his first five books had won him considerable fame and some small measure of financial security, Melville still felt dissatisfied with his work, and in 1851 he published *Moby Dick*, which although a failure in its day, has proved in the twentieth century to be his most famous work.

It was also during these first few years at home following his travels that Melville became established as an important member of the New York literary group, and became a friend of Nathaniel Hawthorne, whose encouragement was of immeasurable aid in the writing of *Moby Dick*. So much so in fact that Melville dedicated the book to him with the following inscription: "In token of my admiration for his genius this book is inscribed to Nathaniel Hawthorne."

In 1847, Melville married Elizabeth Shaw, the daughter of the Chief Justice of Massachusetts, and had in the fall of that year moved from Pittsfield, Massachusetts to New York City. Later, early in 1850, after a brief trip to London to make arrangements for the publication of *White Jacket*, he moved to "Arrowhead," a farm in Pittsfield, Massachusetts where he was to remain for the next thirteen years.

Unfortunately for Melville the critical reaction to *Moby Dick* was negative, and the reaction to *Pierre* (1852), a somewhat confused and melodramatic novel which attacked, among other things, conventional morality and publishing practices, was even worse. Disturbed by his waning popularity and in ill health, Melville turned for a time to writing articles and short stories for the magazines Putnam's and Harper's. Among his works in this period are *Israel Potter* (1855), which had been first published serially, and *Piazza Tales* (1856), a collection of short stories which included the now famous "Bartelby the

Scrivener" and "Benito Cereno." In 1857, he published the last novel in his lifetime, *The Confidence Man*, a satiric tale which has its setting on a Mississippi River steamboat, and which like *Moby Dick* has aroused much recent critical interest.

His career now at its lowest ebb, ill and in debt, Melville traveled through the Mediterranean countries and the Holy Land on borrowed money, and on his return attempted to make his living lecturing on such subjects as "statuary in Rome" and "the South Seas." Unsuccessful, he sold his farm at Pittsfield, paid his debts with the remaining money, and bought a house in New York City where he secured a job in the Custom House which he held until his retirement in 1885.

During these years and those which followed, Melville published several volumes of poetry, including: *Battle Pieces and Aspects of the War* (1866), *Clarel: a Poem and a Pilgrimage in the Holy Land* (1876), *John Marr and Other Sailors* (1888), and *Timoleon* (1891). These last three volumes were for the most part privately printed in small editions at the expense of an uncle, Peter Gansevoort.

At his death on September 28, 1891, Melville left in manuscript a considerable number of verses as well as the short novel, Billy Budd, which was not published until 1924. It has since proved one of his most interesting works, for in addition to accelerating an already reviving interest in Melville, it has achieved much critical acclaim.

MOBY DICK

BRIEF SUMMARY OF MOBY DICK

Moby Dick is told to us by a man who identifies himself only as Ishmael. Impelled by an urge to see more of the world and understand more of its mysteries, Ishmael decides to go to sea. He leaves New York and travels to New Bedford, Massachusetts, where he spends a night with a South Seas cannibal named Queequeg as a roommate. At first frightened by Queequeg, Ishmael soon finds him likeable enough.

While at New Bedford, Ishmael goes to a famous whaleman's chapel whose pastor, Father Mapple, is widely known in the whaling fleet. Father Mapple preaches a sermon which focuses on the story of Jonah and the whale, in which he emphasizes that man must reject his own pride and be true to God, letting no other force guide him. Ishmael and Queequeg become fast friends at New Bedford, and decide to go to Nantucket Island and sign on the same whaleship together. They take a packet boat, and on the trip to Nantucket, Queequeg saves an obnoxious lout from drowning in the icy waters. (This is the first of a number of scenes in which men are saved from drowning.) At Nantucket, Queequeg tells Ishmael that his god has decided that Ishmael must choose the ship on which they will sail, and Ishmael chooses the Pequod because it is so picturesque. Both men sign on, and are told that the ship's captain is Ahab, an unusual man but one who "has his humanities." He is confined at his home because of some mysterious sickness, so Ishmael cannot see him. As Ishmael and Queequeg leave the ship they are accosted by a queer old man who drops dark hints about Ahab.

The ship sails on a cold, gray Christmas day. As the two men approach the Pequod, they see a group of shadowy figures board the ship before them. The ship plunges out into the Atlantic and for many days nothing is seen of Ahab. Ishmael presents the three mates, Starbuck, Stubb, and Flask, then the harpooners, and then describes the crew in general. The ship sails down the Atlantic into a warmer climate, and Ahab finally makes an appearance. As time passes, Ahab appears more frequently, usually standing in one of two holes drilled on the quarter-deck for his peg leg of whalebone. A scene between Ahab and the second mate, Stubb, shows that something is disturbing Ahab profoundly.

Ishmael tells us something of whales, categorizing them according to size and type, and showing why he considers the sperm whale the noblest of all. He also begins to give us what proves ultimately to be an immense amount of information about whales, whaling, whaleships, and whalemen. Then comes the first "big scene" of the book-Ahab calls all the crew onto the quarter-deck, and tells them that he has sworn to hunt to the death the great whale, Moby Dick, that ripped his leg off on his last voyage. He inflames the crew so that except for Starbuck, the first mate, they are all eager to pursue Moby Dick; and he nails a gold doubloon to the mainmast, promising it as a reward for the first man to sight Moby Dick on the voyage.

Ishmael sets himself to find out as much as he can about this whale, and discovers that, besides being unusually large and deformed in certain ways, Moby Dick has a savage temper which has led him to destroy many a whaleboat and kill a number of seamen. He is so ferocious that he seems, unlike ordinary whales, to know what he is doing, and to destroy boats and men with conscious malice. Most frightening of his characteristics, however, is his whiteness, which is mysterious.

As the Pequod moves down the South Atlantic, around the Cape of Good Hope, and across the Indian Ocean, Ahab spends night after night with his charts and maps, tracing on them courses on which he might stand the best chance of meeting Moby Dick. Ishmael continues to fill us in on details of whales and whaling. Several times whales are sighted and chased; at the first lowering it is discovered that Ahab has a special boat crew, led by a Satanic Oriental named Fedallah - this stowaway boat crew explains the mysterious figures Ishmael saw when boarding the ship. The Pequod also meets or has significant contact with nine other vessels in the course of the voyage (the Goney, Town-Ho, Jeroboam, Jungfrau, Bouton-de-rose, Samuel Enderby, Bachelor, Rachel, and Delight). Each one of these ships, by contrast or parallel to the Pequod, gives us new information or a slightly different attitude toward Ahab's ship and his quest. And along with all this, we get Ishmael's constant reflections as the philosophical narrator continually examines his experiences and tries to fathom what they mean and where they are leading.

As the Pequod sails across the Pacific, Ahab becomes ever more intense in his desire to destroy Moby Dick. He asks each one of the ships he encounters, "Hast seen the White Whale?" but it is only when he sails the ship down to the equator that he finally meets a ship which has seen Moby Dick. In the meantime, Pip, a little Negro youth, has been temporarily abandoned in the sea, and has lost his mind before being saved by the ship. Touched by Pip's plight, Ahab has taken special care of him, keeping him in his cabin. Pip begs Ahab several times to abandon his quest for the White Whale, but Ahab, though deeply moved, continues the search.

The suspense of the hunt builds throughout several weeks. The ship meets the Samuel Enderby, whose captain has recently lost his arm to Moby Dick. Ahab cracks his ivory leg leaving the Enderby, and must have a new one made by the ship's carpenter. The Pequod runs into a typhoon, during which the mastheads glow with a mysterious electrical fire. In a weird ritual, Ahab claims to be a son of the fire and lightning, and challenges nature to do its worst to him. Finally the ship meets two whalers, the Rachel and the Delight, which have just had battles with Moby Dick. Despite dire warnings, Ahab presses the chase furiously, and the tension mounts. One last quiet day dawns; Starbuck tries his utmost to convince Ahab that the quest is folly, but Ahab feels that his acts have been foreordained since eternity, and cannot turn back. On the following day Ahab himself sights Moby Dick, thus (ironically) gaining his own promised reward.

The first day the boats approach Moby Dick, but he dives and, coming up under Ahab's boat, bites it in half. The Pequod sails up, drives the whale off, and picks up all its boats; then the ship follows the whale. On the second day, all three whaleboats get harpoons into Moby Dick, but he fights furiously; two boats are smashed and Ahab's is overturned. All are saved except Fedallah (who has predicted that Ahab's death would be preceded by certain signs, among which was to be Fedallah's own death).

On the third day Ahab harpoons the whale, but is left to fight him alone when the other two boats, damaged, are forced to return to the Pequod. Moby Dick breaks loose from Ahab's boat, turns, and dashes his immense forehead into the Pequod's bow. The crushed boat sinks. As it settles, Ahab darts one last harpoon into Moby Dick, but the line catches him around the neck and he is dragged down into the sea. The vortex created by the sinking ship pulls down everything except one lone survivor- Ishmael. He is rescued by the Rachel, which is still cruising the area looking for survivors from its previous encounter with Moby Dick. And the sea rolls on as it did thousands of years ago.

ETYMOLOGY AND EXTRACTS

Melville prefaces *Moby Dick* with a brief list of the words for "whale" in thirteen different languages. Then he adds a list of "Extracts" - brief excerpts - from various references to whales found in literature all over the world. The list embraces references ranging in time from the Old Testament to Melville's contemporaries, and it is drawn from plays, whaling manuals and histories, poetry, essays, books of morality, political writings, grammar-school textbooks, songs, and even a missionary's journal. There are no fewer than eighty of these "Extracts."

Comment

Melville has compiled an extraordinary - and extremely long-list of remarks about the whale here. Why? Because he wishes to impress the reader immediately with the fact that the whale has been known in all lands and at all times. He wants us to realize that the interest which he shows in this gigantic creature is by no means original with him, and that the whale has, since time immemorial, been a symbol of the powerful and mysterious forces of nature. He may also be trying to overwhelm the reader for "effect."

MOBY DICK

TEXTUAL ANALYSIS

CHAPTERS 1-9

CHAPTER I: LOOMINGS

"Call me Ishmael." With these three words, the narrator of *Moby Dick* introduces himself rather mysteriously to the reader, and begins what is probably the greatest sea-story ever written. Ishmael, a landsman (one who is not habitually a sailor) from New York, tells us that "some years ago-never mind how long precisely" he decided to go to sea to drive away a feeling of melancholy and moodiness. This is his way of forgetting the difficulties of life ashore. Let other men commit suicide if they can't face their troubles, but Ishmael will go to sea when, as he puts it, he finds himself "involuntarily pausing before coffin warehouses, and bringing up the rear of every funeral" he meets.

There is nothing unusual about the urge to sail the ocean, Ishmael assures us. Look at the wharves of Manhattan on Sunday afternoon, and you will see thousands of men staring out to sea. Even the island of Manhattan itself is surrounded by water, and its streets lead the stroller toward the water. If we leave Manhattan and go to the country, we still find that water mysteriously attracts men. A country path, in a region of lakes, leads to a pool or stream. The artist painting a landscape includes a stream in his picture. The visitor to the prairies is disappointed because there is no water there. In ancient times, the Greeks and Persians regarded the seas with reverence. (In other words, at all times and in all places, the sea has exercised a strange fascination for the human race.)

Comment

Two important factors are introduced immediately in the opening paragraph:

1. The name "Ishmael" is very significant. Ishmael, in the Bible, was the son of Abraham and a slave woman, Hagar. Sarah, Abraham's wife, insisted that he abandon Hagar and Ishmael, and Ishmael became an outcast. The name is therefore symbolic of the wanderer or displaced person. As we will see many times, Ishmael not only wanders over the world, but is wandering spiritually in search of the meaning of life.

2. Ishmael tells us that the actual events of the story took place years ago-so that many of the comments he makes will refer to things which he couldn't really understand when they first occurred. He is wiser "now" than he was when he took the voyage.

In discussing the ways in which water fascinates men, Ishmael is preparing us for the mysteries of the sea which we will encounter as the voyage unfolds. The voyage is in a sense the voyage journey of life, and the dreams of water which Ishmael thinks haunt most men suggest the great "sea" of life, which the ocean, with all its wonders, represents in this novel.

When Ishmael goes to sea, he never travels as a passenger, because he usually has no money. On the other hand, he wants no part of the duties and responsibilities of being an officer, for it is difficult enough simply to take care of himself when he is out on the ocean. He chooses to ship out as a common sailor, because he gets paid for his work and because the work he does is healthy and fairly active. True enough, he may be ordered around by a dictatorial officer - this is an experience that is very trying for a proud man - but he can stand being treated harshly, because life aboard ship demands rigid discipline, and everyone is under the command of someone else. Even the Commodore who commands the ship is not as free as he thinks he is (Ishmael says, "Who ain't a slave? Tell me that."). Even his air comes to him second-hand - the lowly sailors, stationed toward the bow of the ship, breathe it first.

Ishmael tells us that chose a whaling ship for this voyage, but he cannot explain why. The Fates, he supposes, must have had a hand in his decision. Nonetheless, he admits, he was dazzled by the idea of the whale itself - and had a powerful desire to experience the adventure of seeing the marvelous creature in some remote corner of the world. The whale (like the sea) became such a goad to his imagination, that he felt he had to discover what the reality was like.

Summary

The opening chapter, naturally, helps establish a frame of reference for the whole novel. The point of view of Ishmael will, for much of the story, be our point of view. (Later in the book, Melville shifts the viewpoint several times, and uses a number of different expository and narrative techniques.) The following important notes are introduced in this chapter:

1. We learn the importance of Ishmael's name. Many other names in the book, especially those coming from the Bible (Ahab, for example), will have special significance.

2. The sea and the whale are, for Ishmael at least, mysterious and attractive forces. Throughout the entire novel the significance of both will be discussed.

3. The motif (a major **theme** to be elaborated or developed in a piece of literature) of the coffin is mentioned in Ishmael's reference to "coffin warehouses." Coffins or objects resembling coffins will appear frequently in the book. (For example, the tomblike Spouter Inn of Chapter III is owned by a person with the ominous name of Peter Coffin. A coffin is made for Queequeg, Ishmael's cannibal friend, in Chapter CX.)

4. Ishmael suspects that man's free will may not exist at all. "Ain't we all slaves?" is his comment on life in general, as well as life aboard ship, and his insistence on the role of "those stage managers, the Fates" implies that he thinks man's life may be determined by forces beyond his control.

5. We get a hint as to the importance of objects to Ishmael. Throughout the novel he is constantly ruminating about the meaning of things. (Notice how many of the chapter titles of *Moby Dick* are the names of objects.) The title of this chapter, "Loomings," is itself a hint regarding the rest

of the story, for every major event in the book is prepared for by several "loomings" (as a noun, the word doesn't exist - Melville created it himself), or foreshadowings of future occurrences.

CHAPTER II: THE CARPET-BAG

Stuffing only "a shirt or two" into his carpet-bag, Ishmael leaves Manhattan for New Bedford, Massachusetts, planning to take a ship sailing from Nantucket Island. He feels that it would be unfitting to sail from any other port, for Nantucket is the original home of whaling in America: from that island "those aboriginal whalemen, the Red-Men" first set out in canoes to chase the leviathan. Arriving at New Bedford, Ishmael discovers that he has missed the packet boat to the island, and must spend two nights and a day in New Bedford. He therefore looks for an inn for the night, but cannot find anything appropriate to his finances and his mood. He sees "The Crossed Harpoons" and the "Swordfish," but both look "too jolly and expensive." Nevertheless he must find lodgings, for it is so fiercely cold that there are ten inches of solid ice on the streets.

Ishmael finally comes upon a sign which reads "The Spouter-Inn: Peter Coffin," and decides to try this in even though he has misgivings about a place whose proprietor has such an ominous name. Before entering, however, he reflects upon the contrast between the cold outside and the warmth of the inn, and considers the lot of Lazarus (the Biblical figure who symbolizes the world's unfortunates) and Dives (the Biblical symbol for the wealthy man who shows no love for his impoverished fellow humans). He ponders the physical imperfections of this gloomy inn, and realizes that they remind him of his own imperfections. Ishmael ends his musings with a pun: "no more of this blubbering" (moaning) now; there will be plenty of blubber (whale's fat) later in the book. (Ishmael is a born talker, and he especially likes to play word-games; he loves puns, good, bad, and indifferent.)

Summary

This chapter takes us close to the starting point of Ishmael's voyage, and also gives us further insights into his character. We discover that he is socially conscious (he sympathizes with the downtrodden Lazarus types of the world) and that he has a strong sense of the brotherhood of all men (he implies clearly that Dives went to hell for his failure to aid the desperate Lazarus). Ishmael's concept of brotherhood is quite important during the first twenty chapters of the book, especially regarding Queequeg, whom we shall meet shortly. We also see several examples of the fact that Ishmael's mind works by contrasts-he considers cold and warmth, dark and light, cruelty and kindness, riches and poverty as he wanders about New Bedford. Finally, we discover that Ishmael feels man to be a very imperfect creature struggling along in a world that is perhaps cold, dark, and even unfriendly to him.

CHAPTER III: THE SPOUTER-INN

Ishmael enters the Spouter-Inn, and finds that it is so low and dark that it reminds him of the interior of a condemned ship. What first catches his attention is an extraordinary painting on one side of the entry-a painting so shadowy and grimy that he cannot discern its subject - "a boggy, soggy, squitchy picture truly, enough to drive a nervous man distracted." After speculating for some time about the picture, Ishmael theorizes that it shows a gigantic whale about to plunge bodily onto the masts and deck of a foundering ship. On the opposite wall Ishmael sees a collection of clubs, spears and tools used in the whaling industry, many of them made of the bones and teeth of the whale itself. These ugly weapons cause Ishmael to shudder because of their appearance and their bloody functions. At the back of the inn is the bar, which is entered through an archway made of the jawbone of a whale, "those jaws of swift destruction."

Comment

Melville has deliberately given the story a somewhat disturbing turn. Not only is the inn called "The Spouter" (a "spouter" is, of course, a whale), but one of its doorways is a whale's jaw, the bartender is called a Jonah, there are whale's teeth and bones everywhere, and a picture suggesting the terrifying destructiveness of the whale is immediately evident. To enter "The Spouter-Inn" is, in other words, very much like entering (as did the Jonah of the Bible, who will be the subject of Father Mapple's sermon in Chapter IX) the belly of the whale! Melville is forewarning the reader that the whale and the sea will swallow up men as the story develops.

Ishmael asks Peter Coffin for a room, and is told that he will have to share a bed with a harpooner. Uneasily he accepts the proprietor's terms, and awaits the arrival of his unwelcome roommate. Meanwhile the crew of a newly-returned whaling ship burst into the inn, and the men proceed to get drunk and rowdy. One man alone **refrains** from the revelry, a magnificent giant named Bulkington, who quietly slips out of the inn and disappears. Ishmael will see him again when the two men sail from Nantucket together.

Increasingly ill-at-ease because the harpooner has not yet appeared, Ishmael questions Peter Coffin further and finds that his bed-mate is a South Seas savage who is walking the streets of New Bedford trying to sell his collection of human heads. In an agony of restlessness at this news, Ishmael decides to go to bed quickly and hope that all will be well. Before he can get to sleep, however, his roommate enters, and Ishmael watches in fascination as the man prepares for bed. He is tattooed from head to foot with grotesque figures, he wears a stovepipe hat, and he smokes a pipe which also functions as a tomahawk. Startled to find a stranger in his bed, the savage threatens to brain Ishmael with the tomahawk. Ishmael shouts for help, and a grinning Peter Coffin rushes in to "introduce" him to Queequeg, his bunkmate. After explanations have been made, both men are satisfied, and they settle down to sleep. Ishmael tells us "I ... never slept better in my life."

Summary

The first hints of the real terrors of whaling are given in this chapter. Besides the omens already mentioned, remember the hideous sickle-shaped spear which Ishmael describes in this chapter-Moby Dick's deformed jaw is described as a sickle more than once in the novel. Further, consider Ishmael's reaction to Queequeg ("a man can be honest in any sort of skin" and "Better sleep with a sober cannibal than a drunken Christian") - he attempts to judge Queequeg, and all men, by what they are and do, rather than by what they profess to be. He and Queequeg become spiritual brothers on the voyage, and his willingness to trust Queequeg saves his life, in a sense, at the end of the tale. In this uncertain life, Melville implies, all one can do is choose one's friends according to deep instincts, and then hope for the best. As Ishmael puts it, "I ain't insured" - and no man can be sure of his future.

Note that this chapter, serious though it is, contains several gleams of a rather sardonic humor; Ishmael's first encounter with Queequeg is shot full of comic horror. Humor often appears in the most serious sequences in *Moby Dick* (for instance, in Father Mapple's comical directions in Chapter IX, and Ishmael's rueful comments in Chapter XLIX). Be on guard for such paradoxical humor throughout the novel, and notice its rough-and-ready, folk humor characteristics.

CHAPTER IV: THE COUNTERPANE

Ishmael awakens the next morning to find Queequeg's arm thrown over him. He notices that Queequeg's tattooed arm and the counterpane or quilt blend with each other, so that he can hardly distinguish Queequeg's arm except by its weight. He then reflects upon a peculiar experience of his childhood, in which, having been sent to bed supperless on the longest day of the year, he awoke in the middle of the night feeling that a supernatural hand had been placed in his own. He has never been able to explain this phenomenon to himself. Ishmael is shocked back to actuality by the realization that he has just rolled over on Queequeg's tomahawk, and he begins to push and shout at his companion. Queequeg, at first oblivious to Ishmael's commotion, finally awakens, sits up stiffly, and then leaps out of bed to dress. To Ishmael's astonishment, he first puts on his hat, then crawls under the bed to put on his boots (Queequeg evidently considers this stage of dressing the most personal, and therefore seeks privacy during the operation). After scrambling from under the bed, Queequeg finishes dressing and proceeds to shave with the head of his harpoon.

Summary

Queequeg's hugging Ishmael in a "matrimonial sort of style" foreshadows the friendship, severed only by death, which the two men will share. The oddities of Queequeg's habits serve not only to make him a striking and memorable character, but also show us the breadth of Ishmael's warm and humorous sympathy. The fact that Queequeg shaves with the blade of his harpoon suggests how the incidentals of whaling subtly permeate the whaleman's life and give it a special atmosphere. Finally, Ishmael's mention of his stepmother accentuates his rootlessness, and the "supernatural hand" he felt may reflect a belief that men are sometimes assisted by powers beyond their comprehension.

CHAPTER V: BREAKFAST

Ishmael follows Queequeg downstairs to the breakfast table, and notices Peter Coffin grinning at him. He bears Coffin no grudge for his little joke, because there are too few laughs in the world and he is glad to have been the source of another's harmless enjoyment. As he looks around the table, he notices that he can tell how long a man has been ashore by the degree to which his tan has faded (again, the whaling life leaves its recognizable mark on a man). To his surprise, these amazingly brave and hardy men are shy and ill at ease with one another (presumably because they are "out of their element" when on land). Queequeg alone shows none of this shyness; he reaches the length of the table and spears pieces of beefsteak-Ishmael adds with ironic reference to his supposed cannibalism that Queequeg prefers his steaks very rare-with the ever-present harpoon. After breakfast, Queequeg smokes his pipe while Ishmael goes out for a stroll.

Summary

In this chapter Ishmael continues to show himself a close observer of men and their behavior. He plainly is beginning to admire Queequeg, especially for his calm self-possession under all circumstances. In the whaleboats the harpooner is the all-important figure, and Queequeg's self-assurance shows that he is aware of this relatively exalted position in the world of the whaler. It also suggests the fearlessness which he will demonstrate on many occasions.

Ishmael's willingness to be the butt of a joke parallels his attitude toward being subject to authority ("Who ain't a slave?") in Chapter I. In both the literal and the figurative sense, Ishmael feels that "all men are in the same boat" (the ship he sails on will be a little world in itself). Is he the essence of democracy?

CHAPTER VI: THE STREET

Strolling about the streets of New Bedford, Ishmael realizes that Queequeg is by no means the oddest spectacle to be seen in the whaling industry. Cannibals and savages there are, to be sure - but none of these is any more outlandish than the back-country dandy who decides to go to sea. Ishmael comments wryly on the fancy clothing worn by the Green Mountains bumpkin-clothing which will collapse in a moment under the furious strain of working in a tempest at sea. But New Bedford has its beauties, too-fine parks, streets, and mansions, and blooming young women. None of these would exist in New Bedford, Ishmael implies, if it had not been for the whaling industry.

CHAPTER VII: THE CHAPEL

After returning from his stroll, Ishmael decides to go out again to pay a visit to a special whaleman's chapel in New Bedford. A driving, sleety storm has replaced the fine clear weather of the morning, and the walk to the chapel is difficult and unpleasant. Shaking the sleet from his coat and hat, Ishmael looks around the chapel and notes the austere marble tablets commemorating those who died battling whales. He also notices that the mourners sit apart from one another, deliberately isolated, "as if each silent grief were insular and incommunicable." He is surprised to see Queequeg among those present, especially since Queequeg cannot read the inscriptions in the chapel.

Ishmael sympathizes with the mourners present, for they haven't even the consolation of a grave to visit; their dead lie shrouded in unknown waters thousands of miles away. As he contemplates such a burial, Ishmael naturally reflects that the fate of the whalemen named on those frigid tablets may well be his own, and is temporarily depressed. His spirits rise again, however, for only his body can be killed by a whale-as he concludes, "stave my soul, Jove himself cannot."

Comment

For the second time, Ishmael has come from brutally cold weather into a building which contains unsettling references to the whale. Melville may be suggesting through Ishmael's experiences that the choices facing men (what "elements" shall a man confront?) are all equally unpleasant and dangerous. Be that as it may, Ishmael asserts his absolute independence:

whether a man is free or not, even the Fates cannot destroy his individuality-a man can preserve his integrity regardless of circumstances.

Note that the pagan Queequeg's presence here in the Christian chapel anticipates the situation of Chapter X, in which Ishmael joins in Queequeg's worship of a tiny wooden idol. The code of the brotherhood of man, for Ishmael and Melville, transcends doctrinal considerations.

CHAPTER VIII: THE PULPIT

Shortly after Ishmael takes a seat, a robust old man enters the chapel and advances to the pulpit. This is the chaplain, the famous Father Mapple, a man who was a whaleman and harpooner as a youth, but who has devoted himself to the ministry for many years. Father Mapple's entrance calls Ishmael's attention to the pulpit, which is an extraordinary structure, so high that it reminds Ishmael of the bow of a ship. When Father Mapple starts to ascend to the pulpit by way of a ship's ladder, Ishmael fears momentarily that the chaplain may be a mere performer rather than a sincere preacher, but he concludes that the peculiarity of Mapple's method "must symbolize something unseen." Perhaps, thinks Ishmael, the isolation Mapple achieves in the pulpit severs him from worldly considerations for the moment, making him fitter to lead spiritually. While musing on this matter, Ishmael notices an odd painting on the wall behind the pulpit: it represents a ship sailing against a terrible storm, and shows the face of an angel beaming down upon the scene, throwing a spot of light upon the ship's deck. Ishmael reflects that "the storm of God's quick wrath" is first seen from the pulpit, and that "the world's a ship on its passage out, and not a voyage complete; and the pulpit is its prow."

Comment

This chapter suggests three major considerations:

1. The problem of isolation-is it good or bad to be isolated from others? Mapple's isolation, presumably, is good - what of others who are "alone" in the book?

2. The mysterious picture behind the pulpit contrasts directly with that seen in the Spouter-Inn-are we seeing two contrasted possible outcomes for the "stormy voyage of life?"

3. The man in high place - the leader, whether he be chaplain or captain - sees "God's wrath" first. What will he do about it? Captain Ahab's reaction will be anticipated, in some ways, by Father Mapple's sermon on Jonah in the next chapter.

CHAPTER IX: THE SERMON

As Ishmael watches, Father Mapple gives brisk directions to his scattered congregation: "Starboard gangway ... to larboard-larboard gangway to starboard! Midships! Midships!" The worshippers all move to the center of the chapel, and Mapple begins his sermon. First he says a brief prayer, and then leads his congregation in a hymn expressing Jonah's fears in the belly of the whale which swallowed him. The hymn ends on the note of joy Jonah felt when he was delivered from the whale (Ishmael tells us that the hymn "swelled high above the howling of the storm"). Mapple then proceeds into a powerful discourse on Jonah's attempt to flee from God, stressing that Jonah's sin "was in his wilful disobedience of the command of God ... which he found a hard command." Mapple warns that all God's commands are difficult, and that we must disobey ourselves-a difficult task-if we are to obey God.

Comment

Father Mapple's insistence that the group in the chapel gather together does two things: it suggests the need of unity (in Chapter VII Ishmael noted the isolation of the mourners) among men if any worthy end is to be achieved, and it anticipates Captain Ahab's gathering of the crew on the quarter-deck, for very different purposes, in Chapter XXXVI. The hymn which is sung stresses conflict between man and whale - but Jonah calls on God and is saved. In his conflict with the whale, Ahab will refuse to turn to any God but himself (we shall see with what results). Ishmael mentions that the hymn drowns out the storm: is he (or Melville) suggesting that faith, such as Ahab will fail to demonstrate, can triumph over the forces which buffet men about the world?

Mapple tells his listeners that Jonah tries to flout God by fleeing from Him on a ship, hoping to reach "countries where God does not reign." He mentions a poster on the wharf from which Jonah plans to leave: the poster offers five hundred gold coins for a man who murdered his father. (This is a minor detail here, but notice how exactly it foreshadows Ahab's offer of the gold doubloon, in Chapter XXXVI, to the first man who sights Moby Dick!) Jonah goes aboard ship, and proceeds below decks where he watches the lamp in his cabin distort all that he sees around him. The ship sails, runs into a tremendous storm, and seems about to founder, when the mariners decide to heave Jonah (whom they consider bad luck) into the sea. As soon as they do so a great whale swallows up Jonah, and the sea calms. Jonah, in the whale's belly, prays for deliverance and is saved after three days. Mapple concludes his sermon by drawing a moral from Jonah's adventure: man must repent for the evil he has done, and he must "preach the Truth to the face of Falsehood." "Woe to him who would not be true, even though to be false were salvation," says Mapple, and "Delight is to him ... who against the proud gods and commodores of this earth, ever stands forth his own inexorable self."

Summary

This is one of the key chapters in the book. Father Mapple's sermon anticipates - in reverse - Ahab's basic course of action throughout the book. Ahab will not disobey himself to obey a different "law" - he will sail to the ends of the earth on what seems to be an ungodly mission - he will skulk below decks, like Jonah, at the start of the voyage - he will, like Jonah, see a distorted world by the swinging lamp in his cabin, especially as he reads his charts in Chapter XLIV. (Jonah's swinging lamp is the first of a great many important light, fire, and lightning images in the novel. It prefigures almost exactly Ahab's lamp, which should be compared to the sun in Chapter XXXVII. The culminating point, in many ways, for the fire-and-light images is the try-works scene of Chapter XCVI: here Ishmael will discuss the vital difference between "true" and "false" light.)

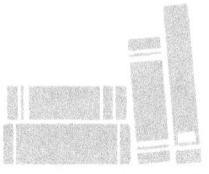

MOBY DICK

TEXTUAL ANALYSIS

CHAPTERS 10-29

CHAPTER X: A BOSOM FRIEND

Returning to the Spouter-Inn, Ishmael finds Queequeg silently whittling at the nose of his little wooden idol, "Yojo." He watches Queequeg carefully, and concludes that there is something naturally admirable about him despite the grotesque tattooing on his face - "You cannot hide the soul," says Ishmael, and Queequeg seems to have a noble soul. He is twenty thousand miles from home, yet he preserves his own dignity and individuality, completely self-sufficient in an alien culture. Ishmael's heart goes out to this solitary savage, and he strikes up a conversation with him. They look through a book together, and Queequeg is taken by Ishmael's friendliness. The two smoke a pipe together, whereupon Queequeg presses his forehead against Ishmael's and announces that they are "married," that is, that they are now lifelong friends. He gives Ishmael several gifts, and then divides his money and gives half to Ishmael. The two go to their room, where Queequeg offers his evening worship to Yojo. Ishmael stretches his Christian conscience slightly and joins in the prayers, feeling that God would want him to follow the golden rule regarding Queequeg's request that he pray with him. After the prayers, the two retire to bed, "a cosy, loving pair."

Comment

The self-sufficiency which Queequeg demonstrates here will appear several times later in the book. The promise Queequeg makes, that he will die for Ishmael if necessary, is of great significance at the novel's conclusion. It is perhaps worthy of note that this chapter is taken by a few critics of *Moby Dick* to adumbrate a **theme** of "innocent homosexual love" which, in their opinion, shows itself from time to time throughout the novel.

CHAPTER XI: NIGHTGOWN

Ishmael and Queequeg nap and chat in bed for some time, but become restless in the middle of the night. Ishmael reflects upon the phenomenon that he doesn't appreciate the warmth of bed unless part of him is cold (showing once more how consistently his mind works in terms of contrasts). Once again the two men light up Queequeg's tomahawk pipe, and, sitting up in bed, Queequeg begins to tell Ishmael his life story.

CHAPTER XII: BIOGRAPHICAL

Queequeg tells Ishmael that he comes from Kokovoko, an island in the South Pacific. His father was a great chief, a king (Queequeg's bearing throughout the book shows his royal lineage), and others of his family also have demonstrated innate nobility. As a young man, Queequeg won passage to the western and Christian world by his persistence - he boarded a ship and seized a ringbolt on the deck, refusing to let go under any circumstances. Ishmael asks Queequeg if he plans to return to his island home, and Queequeg responds that he will when he feels himself baptized again-he adds that his immediate plan is to go to sea on a whaler, and the two men decide to ship out together and share their luck.

Comment

Queequeg's reference to baptism is interesting and important. The motif of baptism-ritual purification by being submerged in water and then taken from it-will be repeated several times, and Queequeg will be "Baptizer-in-chief." This motif is extremely important, and a variation upon it will conclude the novel.

CHAPTER XIII: WHEELBARROW

The following morning Ishmael and Queequeg settle their account with Peter Coffin and prepare to sail to Nantucket. They rent a wheelbarrow to cart their belongings to the Nantucket schooner, and while walking to the dock Queequeg tells Ishmael that when he first used a wheelbarrow, he had carried both the barrow and its contents on his head! When Ishmael laughs at this absurdity, Queequeg tells another anecdote, this one of a ship's captain who was guilty of a ridiculous breach of propriety at a South Seas wedding feast. All parts of the world have usages which are likely to seem odd or laughable to strangers.

> **Comment**

These stories of Queequeg's, suggesting the relativity of values, foreshadow Queequeg's heroic deed later in the chapter.

The two men board the schooner, which sails briskly, out of New Bedford. A stupid passenger makes fun of Queequeg's odd appearance, and Queequeg, without visible anger, throws the bumpkin up into the air, causing him to turn a somersault and land on the deck on his feet. Just as the captain arrives to scold Queequeg, a boom on the ship's mast breaks loose, knocking the oafish passenger overboard and threatening to capsize the little ship. Queequeg singlehandedly lassoes the terrifying boom (which Ishmael suggests looks like "the lower jaw of an exasperated whale" - still another use of the whale as a point of reference for the significance of seemingly isolated episodes), and then leaps overboard to save the buffoon from drowning in the icy waters. After he has been dried off and warmed up a bit, Queequeg is quite casual about his heroism, as if he were saying to himself, "It's a mutual, joint-stock world. ... We cannibals must help these Christians."

> **Comment**

The major event of this chapter, Queequeg's rescue of the clownish greenhorn, is an example of the "baptism motif" referred to in the summary of the preceding chapter (look for this motif especially in Chapter LXXVIII and in the epilogue). The relativity of values stressed in Queequeg's anecdotes anticipates the fact that Queequeg, when a man's life is at stake, forgets that the victim has insulted him only moments earlier, and risks his own life to save that of a man whom he might have considered his enemy. Fittingly, the ship's captain is forced to reverse judgment of Queequeg; he makes an apology to this noble "cannibal."

CHAPTER XIV: NANTUCKET

The two companions arrive at Nantucket without further adventure. Ishmael reflects on the nature and the history of this barren island, and remarks that it is no wonder the Nantucketers took to the sea for a living. He especially concentrates his musings on the whale, "that Himmalehan, salt-sea mastodon" of "unconscious power" (contrast Ishmael's "unconscious" power to the kind of power Ahab feels Moby Dick represents). Ishmael suggests that the Nantucketer alone lives out of the ocean proper, whereas most sailors and merchants merely use the sea as a means of transportation for goods that are essentially foreign to the ocean.

CHAPTER XV: CHOWDER

The packet boat arrives at Nantucket well after dark, creating difficulties for Ishmael and Queequeg in their search for the "Try Pots," the inn which Peter Coffin has recommended to them. They find the place eventually, however, and seat themselves in hopes of a fine meal. They are not disappointed, as the proprietor's wife brings them steaming bowls of both clam and codfish chowder. Ishmael banters good-naturedly with the woman until he and Queequeg decide to turn in. The two friends go to bed after Queequeg has left his harpoon (a weapon with which one harpooner committed suicide at the Try Pots) downstairs with Mrs. Hussey, the owner's wife.

CHAPTER XVI: THE SHIP

Queequeg informs Ishmael that the little idol, Yojo, has decided that Ishmael must choose the ship on which the two men should sail, Ishmael does not care for the plan, but Queequeg refuses to run counter to Yojo's wishes, so the next morning, while Queequeg observes a Ramadan, or day of fasting and prayer, Ishmael sets out to find a ship. There are three vessels preparing for long whaling voyages: the Devil-Dam, the Tit-Bit, and the Pequod. The Pequod fascinates him because of its ancient, noble, and "bearded" look (the romantic aspects of the Pequod attract him, as the romantic aspects of whaling do). Most interesting of all, the ship is a "cannibal of a craft ... her unpanelled, open bulwarks were garnished like one continuous jaw." Looking about the worn quarter-deck, Ishmael sees a little tent-like structure, in which he encounters Captain Peleg, a crotchety old man who is part owner of the Pequod. Peleg scoffs at Ishmael's limited experience as a seaman on a merchant vessel (whalemen consider merchantmen weak-kneed sailors), and deflates his romantic urge to "see the world" by pointing out that all he will see on a whaling ship is water-which he can see from the dock.

Ishmael next meets Captain Bildad, another part-owner of the ship, a quiet, unobtrusive, but cold person. He reflects that both Peleg and Bildad (both names come from the Bible) - and many other Nantucket whalemen - are Quakers, "fighting Quakers," such men as may well be "formed for noble tragedies ... "Quakers with a vengeance." (Note these remarks and apply them to Captain Ahab, who is a Quaker formed for tragedy and quite literally a "Quaker with a vengeance." Melville is giving the reader "loomings" again.) Peleg rages briefly against Bildad's miserly proposal that Ishmael be given the seven hundred and seventy-seventh lay - that is, one-seven hundred and seventy-seventh of the profits from the voyage - and signs Ishmael on the crew for the three hundredth lay. Ishmael mentions Queequeg and his skill to Peleg, and Peleg tells him to bring the harpooner down to the ship to sign up. As he is leaving, Ishmael asks to see Ahab, and is told that Ahab is at home and will not see anyone at present. He is informed that Ahab is an extraordinary man, "above the common," a hard taskmaster but a man who "has his humanities." (His young wife and child prove that he is not an unloving person.) It is also revealed that he has lost one leg. Ishmael mentions that the Ahab of the Bible was an evil man, though a king, to which Peleg replies that Ahab is basically good - "yet the old squaw, Tistig, at Gayhead, said the name would somehow prove prophetic." Ishmael departs, vaguely sympathetic and sorrowful for Ahab.

Summary

Several important developments occur in this chapter:

1. The ship is chosen (note that the Pequods were a tribe of Indians annihilated by the Puritans in the seventeenth century).

2. The Pequod is a "cannibal," decked out like a whale's jawbone (as in the Spouter-Inn, Ishmael has walked into the whale's jaws!).

3. An ominous tone is developed in the discussion of Ahab's character.

4. Another motif - that of the prophetic character-is introduced with Peleg's reference to the aged Indian squaw who foretold that Ahab's name would eventually

prove significant. (Two major examples of the "prophet figure" are seen in Chapters XIX, XXI, and LXXI).

CHAPTER XVII: THE RAMADAN

Ishmael returns to the inn, but out of respect for Queequeg's Ramadan he decides not to disturb his friend until dark. When he knocks on the door at evening. Queequeg fails to answer, and the silence within continues even though Ishmael creates a disturbance, banging and shouting in the hallway. Mrs. Hussey notices that Queequeg's harpoon is missing, and frantically concludes that he has killed himself. Ishmael breaks open the door, and finds Queequeg doing penance squatting in the middle of the floor with Yojo on his head. He will not respond to Ishmael's worried questions - nor does he do so at bedtime, when Ishmael asks him to take something to eat. Only when the sun shines into the room early next morning does Queequeg arise from this torturous position.

Ishmael, convinced that Queequeg's behavior amounts to religious fanaticism, tries to persuade Queequeg that his practices are in error, but Queequeg can understand only a little of Ishmael's argument, and pays no attention to what he does understand. The two simply decide to "live and let live," and go down to the ship after an unusually hearty breakfast.

CHAPTER XVIII: HIS MARK

As Ishmael and Queequeg approach the Pequod, Captain Peleg shouts that the savage will not be allowed aboard unless he can produce papers showing him to be a Christian. For a moment this seems an impossible difficulty, but Ishmael's earnest argument that Queequeg belongs to the original "ancient Catholic Church" ("catholic" means universal-in other words, Queequeg belongs not to a specific sect, but to the brotherhood of the human race) persuades the good-natured Peleg that, in this case, papers won't be necessary.

Queequeg is asked if he has ever harpooned a whale. Instead of answering, he leaps atop a bulwark, points to a tiny spot of tar on the water, and drives it under with a perfect "dart" or throw of his harpoon. Excited by such astounding skill, Peleg signs him on immediately, calling him Quohog" (a simple clam, especially common in Nantucket) rather than Queequeg. The contrast between the man of action (Peleg) and the contemplative man (Bildad) is stressed when Bildad, instead of showing pleasure at recruiting such a man, gloomily gives Queequeg a Quaker religious pamphlet.

CHAPTER XIX: THE PROPHET

As Ishmael and Queequeg leave the Pequod, they are accosted by a shabby, wild-looking old man who asks them, "Shipmates, have ye shipped in that ship?" Ishmael admits that they have done so, whereupon the stranger reels off a series of incoherent but vaguely frightening remarks about what has happened to Ahab in the past-references to "that thing that happened to him off Cape Horn" and "that deadly skrimmage with the Spaniard afore the altar in Santa, "as well as "his losing his leg last voyage, according to the prophecy." Ishmael insists that the man come to the point but he is evasive, saying only "What's to be will be. ... Morning to ye, shipmates, morning." Before they part, however, the old man tells Ishmael that his name is Elijah (an Old Testament prophet's name). The man follows them for some time but finally disappears, and Ishmael concludes that he is a fraud.

> **Comment**

In this chapter we encounter further unsettling hints about Ahab, but there is still nothing clearly stated. Not only are Elijah's remarks vague and rather incoherent; the old man himself, it seems, may well be crazy. Surely we're not going to take his innuendoes seriously-or are we?

> **CHAPTER XX: ALL ASTIR**

The period of preparation for sailing is one of tremendous activity for a whaler. The Pequod is going on a three year's voyage-it might even be longer - and an enormous quantity of supplies is necessary. Immense amounts of food, spare parts, and materials for repairs are taken aboard, as well as the barrels needed to store whale oil. Ishmael and Queequeg decide to remain ashore as long as possible, but visit the ship daily to observe the preparations. Ishmael is amused by the activity of Captain Bildad's sister, Aunt Charity, who brings aboard such items as jars of pickles. Ishmael asks about Ahab several times, but receives evasive answers. He has misgivings about sailing for three years under a man he has never seen.

At last the ship is ready to sail.

> **CHAPTER XXI: GOING ABOARD**

At dawn, Ishmael and Queequeg approach the Pequod through the misty air. Ishmael remarks some shadows, which seem to be sailors, hurrying toward the ship. Suddenly Elijah appears out of the mist with a shout, asking if they plan to board the vessel.

When Ishmael assures him that they do, Elijah tantalizingly asks them how soon they plan to return, and infers that they may not come back at all. He tells them to see if they can find the four or five figures which boarded the ship a moment earlier, and then disappears with one last suggestion that they may not see each other again. Ishmael concludes that Elijah is "cracked," and he and Queequeg go on board and down to the forecastle (the compartment at the bow), where they have a smoke. The fragrance of the smoke awakens a lone sleeper there, who tells them that Ahab has come aboard and has vanished into his cabin. Then the voice of Starbuck, the first mate, is heard, and soon seamen begin to arrive in twos and threes.

Comment

Elijah's final appearance here reiterates his earlier ominous warning in Chapter XIX. The mysterious figures Ishmael sees will appear again, dramatically, at the first lowering in Chapter XLVIII, and their "shadowy" quality will be significant.

CHAPTER XXII: MERRY CHRISTMAS

About noon those who are not making the voyage leave the Pequod, a sign that all is in readiness. Captain Peleg tells Starbuck to order the men to their posts, and begins to order them about ferociously. Bildad, who will pilot the ship out of the harbor, stations himself at the bow to perform his chore. With considerable ado the anchor is raised (Ishmael receives his first kick as a seaman while helping raise it), and the Pequod heads toward open water. By dark the ship is well offshore, and Peleg and Bildad bid a slow, sentimental farewell to their ship and their friends. It is a freezing winter night as the ship plunges "like fate into the lone Atlantic."

Comment

The title of the chapter is obviously ironic - this is hardly a merry Christmas day. But just how ironic the title is will become clear only later, when the reader has rhea opportunity to compare the nature of Ahab's aim with the religious suggestiveness of a voyage which commences on Christmas.

CHAPTER XXIII: THE LEE SHORE

As the Pequod heads farther heads out to sea, Ishmael glances toward the stern to see who the helmsman is. To his astonishment, it is none other than Bulkington, the colossus who so interested him back at the Spouter-Inn. Here is a man who, like the ships he sails in, must avoid the shore. (Ishmael presents us with the paradox of the personality which, in order to preserve itself, must "head out" from safety and security. Ishmael says that "all deep earnest thinking is but the intrepid effort of the soul to keep the open independence of her sea.")

Comment

Ishmael (and Melville?) openly admire the courageous independence of Bulkington, who will not be a slave. But his attitude toward Ahab, who likewise asserts his absolute independence, is ambiguous. Are we to draw the line anywhere, or is all individualism, no matter how extreme, admirable in its own right?

CHAPTER XXIV: THE ADVOCATE

Ishmael plays advocate for the whaling industry in this chapter, hoping to demonstrate that it is as honorable a calling as any of the more respected professions. Whaling is butchery, it is true - but so is the highest military art, says Ishmael. Whaling has wide-reaching economic significance; they have led the world in the exploration of remote regions; whalemen were the first to break through the despotism of Spain. Whaling has a literary history-whalemen have shown themselves to have "good blood" - the whale has been specially set aside as a "royal fish" - on and on Ishmael goes, defending the trade he loves and admires from would-be detractors. He ends by commenting that, if he should by chance leave a precious manuscript to the world after his death, all the credit should go to the whaling trade, for the whaleship was his university. (We can attribute Ishmael's remarks here to Melville himself without any risk of unjustifiable "reading in" of biography where it has no place.)

CHAPTER XXV: POSTSCRIPT

Ishmael adds one conjecture as an afterthought to the preceding "defense" of whaling: what kind of oil is used to anoint kings and queens at coronation ceremonies? What type could possibly be used but the noblest and sweetest of all, the natural oil of the sperm whale?

CHAPTER XXVI: KNIGHTS AND SQUIRES

The first mate of the Pequod, Starbuck, is a thirty-year old Quaker from Nantucket. He is a thin, leathery man of excellent health, tough and sturdy enough to adapt to any climate and to survive vast amounts of physical strain. Unlike many men in the whale fishery he is extremely brave without being in the least foolhardy. Starbuck thinks, "I am here in this critical ocean to kill whales for my living, and not to be killed by them for theirs," and he acts upon this principle when in a whaleboat. He has a basic weakness despite his bravery, however: his devoutness tends toward superstition. He can conquer any physical fear, but he is the type of man, Ishmael tells us, who "cannot withstand those more terrific, because more spiritual terrors, which sometimes menace you from the concentrating brow of an enraged and mighty man."

Ishmael doesn't wish to abase Starbuck, for he believes that whereas men in the mass may be hopelessly corrupt, man in the ideal is a grand and noble creature (this view probably explains Ishmael's reaction to Queequeg). Ishmael wishes to make it clear that if, later in the story, he attributes noble qualities to base individuals, it is because the "great democratic God" gives even to the lowliest moments of greatness.

Comment

The description of Starbuck's character which Ishmael gives us in this chapter is premonitory of Starbuck's future encounters with Ahab-in a strained sense, Starbuck's "superstitiousness" may be called his tragic flaw.

CHAPTER XXVII: KNIGHTS AND SQUIRES

The Pequod's second mate is a careless, good-natured man from Cape Cod named Stubb. Stubb is always smoking a pipe (he keeps a rack full of pipes, fully loaded, as close to him as possible), even when about to harpoon a whale, and he dearly loves physical comfort. The third mate is a stocky, aggressive man named Flask, who comes from Martha's Vineyard (a small island south of Cape Cod). He is utterly without fear or respect for the whale; to him "the wondrous whale was but a species of magnified mouse." The three mates command the three whaleboats when the chase for whales is on. Ishmael compares each mate to a medieval knight who has a squire in attendance - the "squires" in this case being the harpooners. Starbuck chooses Queequeg for his boat, Stubb chooses Tashtego, an Indian from Gay Head (the west end of Martha's Vineyard), and Flask's harpooner is Daggoo, an immense African Negro. The rest of the crew consists of men from all over the world.

Comment

Melville's chapter title openly invites us to compare the mates and harpooners - and the rest of the Pequod's complement - with the heroic characters of ancient romance and **epic**. The polyglot crew, as will become increasingly apparent later, symbolizes loosely all men, and the ship is a kind of "microsom" - a little world in itself.

CHAPTER XXVIII: AHAB

Nothing is seen of the captain for some time after the Pequod puts out of Nantucket-he remains constantly in his cabin (recall the behavior of Jonah in Mapple's sermon). Ishmael surveys the deck for Ahab everytime he goes topside, but never sees him until the ship is well south of the savage North Atlantic winter. Then one moderate morning Ahab is suddenly there on the quarter-deck. He is a big man, apparently in good health, who looks as though he were "made of solid bronze." Two physical deformities are evident: a tremendous, livid scar which runs from his cap to his collar, and an ivory leg made of a whale's jawbone. He stands facing determinedly out over the ship's bow, with his ivory leg fixed in one of two small holes bored for him on the quarter-deck.

Every morning after this first appearance, Ahab can be seen by the crew, sitting, standing or pacing on his quarter-deck. Eventually the weather becomes so fine as to chase away some of the many clouds which Ishmael notices on his brow.

Comment

Melville naturally tries to make Ahab's first appearance a powerful one, after building tension by keeping Ahab out of the novel for so long. Notice that he does not weaken the effect by having Ahab do or say anything: his mere presence is potent enough. Ishmael tells us that an old Manxman predicts that Ahab will never die peacefully - another prophet figure is here at work.

One question is of interest for this chapter: is there something especially fitting about the fact that Ahab's leg, torn off by a whale's jaw, is replaced by part of a whale's jaw?

Note especially the Biblical significance of Ahab's name: Ahab was an evil king of Israel who introduced the worship of pagan gods into his country. He was a fine warrior, but he was killed in battle, and when he was buried, dogs drank his blood.

CHAPTER XXIX: ENTER AHAB; TO HIM, STUBB

As the days roll by, the weather becomes truly beautiful. Ahab is tormented by sleeplessness (perhaps for other reasons than the silence of the sea at night) and spends much of the nights on deck. Forgetting one night that his three mates sleep immediately below the quarter deck, he begins to pace restlessly and awakens Stubb, who ascends and suggests that Ahab's thumping ivory leg might be muffled. Ahab, enraged suddenly, berates him and snarls, "Down, dog, and kennel!" Stubb reacts in anger, but for a reason he cannot fathom-certainly not from fear-he retreats back to his cabin and wonders whether he should mount up to the deck again and strike Ahab, or get down on his knees and pray for him. He muses on a remark made by the cabin boy that Ahab's hammock is frightfully hot in the morning, and assumes that Ahab has "what some folks ashore call a conscience." He also wonders why Ahab goes down into the cargo hold every night. Stubb doesn't worry about the incident for long, however: a pleasure-lover, he decides to go to sleep and forget the whole affair.

Comment

Besides the obvious insight this chapter gives us into Ahab's violent and tormented character, three interesting notes are struck:

1. Stubb simply decides to ignore Ahab's condition (He says, "Think not, is my eleventh commandment") - he is a type, the man who doesn't think too hard about anything. (Ahab, of course, apparently thinks too much.)

Compare Stubb's reaction to Ahab with the reaction of others, especially Starbuck and Ishmael, the thinkers.

2. Ahab is seen as "a hot old man" - the inner fire which abounds in the book.

3. The reference to Ahab's trips to the hold forewarns us of the surprise forthcoming in Chapter XLVIII.

Note also that, for the first time in the book, Melville goes outside the mind of the narrator, Ishmael, for the "facts" of his story.

MOBY DICK

TEXTUAL ANALYSIS

CHAPTERS 30-45

CHAPTER XXX: THE PIPE

After Stubb's departure Ahab leans on the railing for a while, then decides to have a smoke. He lights his pipe and puffs on it for a few minutes, then realizes that he no longer derives any pleasure from smoking. Remarking that his condition is sad indeed when he can't enjoy his pipe, he throws it into the sea. It hisses and disappears.

Comment

Ahab throws overboard, loses, or smashes several objects on the voyage. Each one symbolizes the rejection of some aspect of his connection with the rest of humanity. In this case the loss seems quite small; later the items destroyed are of immense significance.

CHAPTER XXXI: QUEEN MAB

Stubb tells Flask about an odd dream he had after the incident with Ahab. Ahab kicked him with his ivory leg, and when Stubb attempted to kick back his leg came off. An old man came along and told Stubb that he should feel honored to be kicked by Ahab, and Stubb, piqued, offered to kick the old man-whereupon the old man turned around and showed a rump full of marlinspikes. Stubb, wisely decided not to kick so formidable person. Flask simply doesn't know what to think of such a dream. At this point Ahab calls out that there are whales in the vicinity, and tells the crew to look especially for a white whale.

Comment

In his dream, Stubb tells himself that, although to be struck by a man's hand is an insult, to be kicked by a dead ivory leg is not. Is Melville suggesting that Ahab's rage at the mindless whale is senseless? (Later, Starbuck will tell Ahab that Moby Dick attacked him by instinct, and that to seek vengeance on a dumb brute is both nonsensical and blasphemous.) As a minor point, it is interesting to note how very realistic a dream Melville conjured up for his purposes here.

"Queen Mab" (the title) refers to the fairy queen of folklore who produces and guides men's dreams.

CHAPTER XXXII: CETOLOGY

Ishmael decides to provide us with some sound general background about whales. He points out that little has been written about the whale, and much of what has been written is erroneous. He first defines a whale as "a spouting fish with a horizontal tail," scoffing at those who consider it a mammal. Then Ishmael divides all whales into three "books": folio, octavo, and duodecimo. (These names refer to different sizes of books which vary among themselves; suffice it to say here that the folio is large, the octavo much smaller, and the duodecimo smaller yet. Melville seems to have been unaware of an intermediate book size, called a quarto.) There are six "chapters" (types of whales) among the folio group: the sperm whale, right whale, fin-back, humpback, razor back, and sulfur bottom. The octavos consist of five chapters: the grampus, black fish, harwhale, killer, and thrasher. Among the duodecimos there are only three varieties: the huzza porpoise, the Algerine porpoise, and the mealy-mouthed porpoise, Ishmael discusses the name, appearance and characteristics of most of these whales. He ends his discussion of cetology-for the time being-with a reference to a group of whales he considers to be fictitious.

Comment

Through Ishmael, Melville wants seriously to present some accurate information about whales, based on his personal experience. Besides the purely informational aspects of the chapter consider the following points:

1. Ishmael objects to the name "killer whale" on the grounds that all things kill to live. Remember this for future reference, especially during the cook's sermon to the sharks in Chapter LXIV.

2. Ishmael (Melville?) says this book is "but the draught of a draught - that is, Melville is only beginning to explain his view of the world in *Moby Dick*.

3. Ishmael - Melville organizes whales as books. Why - is Melville simply showing an author's whimsy? Perhaps not. Recall that Melville's "Etymology" was supplied by a man who worked in a grammar school; that the "Extracts" were supplied by a "Sub-sub-librarian"; that the entire novel is permeated by references to the whale and descriptions of the whale's body. Melville is apparently trying to make the "stuff" of the whale the "stuff" of the book. In this attempt he is following a principle precious to several of his major contemporaries, notably Emerson, Thoreau, and Whitman, called the "organic principle." These writers attempted to make the form of their works reflect as directly and spontaneously as possible the nature of their subject. Melville's grammarian and librarian seem intended to stress the direct connection between the whale as actuality and the whale as it can be presented through language. Melville's detailed descriptions of the whale are not merely a result of zoological curiosity - they are meaningful reflections of one of the novel's central themes: What is the whale?

CHAPTER XXXIII: THE SPECKSYNDER

Ishmael gives us some information about the relationship between officers and men on a whaleship. The officers sleep toward the stern, the crewmen forward. But the harpooners are an exception because of their special importance to the success of the voyage, and long usage dictates that they will sleep just forward of the captain and mates. Their importance is such that in the early days of whaling a special title, "specksynder," was given to the chief harpooner. Under that title, his function was to oversee all whale-hunting activities, while the captain was limited to the general command of the ship proper.

Ishmael explains that, because a whaler depends for its success upon the hard work of all crewmen, a democratic slackening of rigid shipboard discipline is sometimes found in the whaling fleet. Ahab, for instance, although he expects instant, unquestioning obedience from all his men, demands little from them in the way of formalities. Nevertheless, says Ishmael, he is not above using such formalities "for other and more private ends than they were legitimately intended to subserve." Whatever a man's intellectual superiority, he does not rise to practical leadership unless he uses various expedients, more or less base in themselves, opines Ishmael.

Comment

Besides stressing the already obvious facts of the distinctions between officers and men and the importance of the harpooners, this chapter hints obliquely at Ahab's "private ends," which will become plain in Chapter XXXVI, and increasingly clearer later.

CHAPTER XXXIV: THE CABIN-TABLE

The captain of a ship considers the cabin his personal property, and tradition bears him out. The mates completely accept this tradition, and are extremely docile when, almost as the guests of the captain rather than by right, they arrive there to eat their meals. Protocol dictates that the captain enter and seat himself first, followed by the first, second and third mates, in that order. In leaving the cabin the reverse order is followed, which means that Flask, third mate, sometimes has only a few minutes to bolt his food. He feels that he has never had a full meal since he became an officer (recall Ishmael's remarks in the first chapter about the disadvantages of being an officer). Ahab's cabin is an especially solemn one, for he never talks (therefore, neither do the mates).

By contrast, the harpooners, who eat in the same cabin after the officers have departed, have a hilarious time. They eat heartily and boisterously, and frequently enjoy teasing the cabin boy with threats that they will either scalp him or eat him. Between the ominous silence of Ahab and the savage playfulness of the harpooners, the cabin boy's life is "one continual lip-quiver."

CHAPTER XXXV: THE MAST-HEAD

Ishmael tells us that his first turn to stand watch at the mast-heads comes during very pleasant weather. The function of the mast-head watch is to espy whales, and an American whaleship usually mans the mast-head from the time it leaves port until its very last barrel is filled with whale oil.

Comment

Ishmael immediately launches into reflections about "mast-heads standers" who have nothing to do with whaling: Egyptian astronomers, Saint Simon Stylites (the Christian hermit who lived atop a rock pillar), even the builders of the Tower of Babel. Once again he is connecting the operations of whaling with the whole history of mankind - this time suggesting a vague connection between standing a mast-head and reaching, whether successfully or not, for almost superhuman achievements.

Generally, standing mast-head watches is completely uneventful in such a peaceful sea as the South Pacific, Ishmael informs us. The only great inconvenience lies in the fact that American whalers have no crow's nest, and the watch must stand perched precariously on the narrow crosstrees high up the mast. This is especially dangerous for such a sailor as Ishmael confesses himself to be-a dreamy, thoughtful young man "with the problem of the universe revolving in me." Daydream once too often, and a man may plunge into the quiet summer sea from one hundred feet up, and never be seen again.

Comment

Ishmael insists upon paralleling the physical dangers of a revery at the mast-head and the psychological dangers of the "sunken-eyed young Platonist" (the idealist philosopher) or the Pantheist who naively commits himself to one simplified view of the world and plunges himself into the bottomless, unsearchable "mystic ocean" of reality. More and more, Ishmael is making whaling the **metaphor** for his search for an understanding of life.

CHAPTER XXXVI: THE QUARTER-DECK

One morning, not long after he has thrown away his pipe, Ahab paces the deck more restlessly and intensely than usual. He goes to his cabin for a time, then returns to the deck, and continues to pace ferociously. Suddenly, near sunset, he orders Starbuck to command all the men aft - an extraordinary event on shipboard. When the crew is assembled, Ahab asks them what they do when they see a whale - and what next? - and after that? The men shout their answers as some strange energy of Ahab's transmits itself to them. When he has them thoroughly excited,

Ahab suddenly produces a sixteen dollar gold piece, nails it to a mainmast with a sledge hammer, and announces that it will become the property of the first man to sight a certain white whale. Tashtego, Daggoo, and Queequeg have all seen this whale-it is the famous Moby Dick.

Comment

Superb leader and propagandist that he is, Ahab has led the men perfectly to the precise pitch of excitement which he desires. His overbearing personality is here brought into play for the first time, along with his flair for the dramatic.

Starbuck asks Ahab if Moby Dick is not the whale that tore his leg off. Ahab says that he is, and that he will chase him "round perdition's flames" for revenge. When Starbuck disputes the logicality of Ahab's desire for revenge, the Captain responds with his philosophy: "All visible objects, man, are but as pasteboard masks. ... in each event. ... some unknown but still reasoning thing puts forth the mouldings of its features from behind the unreasoning mask." He sees in Moby Dick "outrageous strength, with an inscrutable malice sinewing it." Starbuck, overwhelmed by Ahab's intensity and the savage joy of the crew at Ahab's announcement, acquiesces, and can only say "God keep me!-keep us all!"

Comment

Finally we see clearly what Ahab has had in mind from the start. He believes that the world is controlled by a vicious intelligence which operates through visible objects, and for him all the viciousness of that evil intelligence is represented by Moby Dick. We now begin to understand why Ishmael - our narrator who has already had the experiences he is describing - has been so interested in what whales "mean."

Ahab passes around a huge mug of grog, and the crewmen drink to their quest for Moby Dick. He seizes the crossed lances of the three mates, who are gathered around him, trying to charge them with his fierce energy. Then he orders the harpooners to remove the heads of the harpoons from their shafts, pours the grog into the inverted ends of the hollow heads, and commands them to drink from the "murderous chalices" with this oath: "God hunt us all, if we do not hunt Moby Dick to his death!" The refilled mug goes around the crew again; then Ahab sends the crew back to their posts.

Comment

The conclusion of this chapter clearly presents a blasphemous **parody** of a religious ritual, underscoring the enormity of Ahab's purpose. His is essentially a religious goal - whether all evil, good, or neither remains to be decided.

CHAPTER XXXVII: SUNSET

Ahab sits in his cabin, watching the wake of the Pequod and contemplating the sinking sun. He considers the torment of his driving urge to destroy Moby Dick, and regrets that he can no longer enjoy beauty. Then he ponders the ease with which he persuaded the crew, with the exception of Starbuck, to join wholeheartedly in the quest for Moby Dick. Suddenly he bursts out in scorn against the gods, "Come forth from behind your cotton bags" (recall "pasteboard masks"), prophesying that he will destroy Moby Dick and repeating that he will not be deterred from his purpose.

Comment

This is a most meaningful chapter from the technical viewpoint. For one thing it is filled with images of confinement-circles (the sea is a goblet with a rim; Ahab's head is enclosed and weighed down with an iron crown; Ahab's "cogged circle" fits the "various wheels" of the crew), contrasted with images of self-direction-straight lines (the Pequod's wake, the sun's dive, the iron rails on which Ahab's "soul is grooved to run" to its purpose). Images of heat and fire, and of fire in connection with water, appear several times here, and will appear over and over hereafter. Keep this little chapter in mind when you read Chapter XLIV, "The Chart."

CHAPTER XXXVIII: DUSK

Starbuck, leaning against the mainmast, reflects fearfully on Ahab's triumph over the crew. He feels he has been conquered by a madman who is a despot to inferiors, but who "would be a democrat to all above" (that is, who would put himself on a level with god or the fates). He hopes that there is still time to change Ahab's views-after all, Moby Dick has the whole world to swim in in order to avoid Ahab - but he fears that he must help Ahab to an evil and self-destructive goal. He hears a burst of laughter from the forecastle and recalls how savage the heathenish crew is. It is typical of the world, as Starbuck sees it, that such violent animal energy as the crew represents should be directed by a brooder like Ahab. Starbuck begs the "blessed influences" for strength to withstand Ahab's aims.

Comment

Note that in this chapter and the two which follow, Melville uses stage techniques giving stage directions and even, in XL, assigning speeches by name to various characters.

CHAPTER XXXIX: FIRST NIGHT-WATCH

Stubb stands alone at the foremast, mending a brace. He wonders about the Pequod's future, and decides that the best thing to do is to laugh off the problem. No matter what happens, he will take comfort in the "fact" (for him) that "it's all predestinated" - the future is predetermined, and man can do nothing about it.

CHAPTER XL: MIDNIGHT, FORECASTLE

The seamen and harpooners are gathered together in the crew's quarters. The crew (as Starbuck has already noted) are carousing; they have been drinking, and are dancing and singing in a dangerously playful mood. As the revelry continues a storm blows up. A Spanish sailor insults Daggoo and the two are about to brawl when one of the mates calls all hands aloft to take in sails (so that the raging storm will not tear them away.)

> **Comment**

This chapter presents a number of parallelisms between the unrest aboard the Pequod and the external "unrest" of nature. A few examples are:

1. The white lightning in the sky is compared to Ahab's symbolic scar.

2. The row (fight) in the forecastle is compared to the row (storm) in the sky. Tashtego says, "Gods and men-both brawlers!"

3. The ring formed for the fight between the Spaniard and Daggoo is paralleled to "the ringed horizon" by the old Manxman. (He says, "In that ring Cain struck Abel," suggesting that men have violated the idea of brotherhood since the beginning of time.)

CHAPTER XLI: MOBY DICK

Ishmael confesses that he was (at least at first) one of the men who joined feverishly in Ahab's search for Moby Dick. He tries to learn as much as he can about the great whale, and he discovers that Moby Dick apparently travels alone (most whales travel in "schools" or groups), that is widely known in the whale fishery, although relatively few whalers have actually chased him, and that he is furiously destructive. He has maimed or killed many of his pursuers, so that those who have met him want to avoid him in the future-except for Ahab.

Ishmael discusses some of the legends which have developed concerning the sperm whale generally. The most powerful and dangerous of whales, it is a "southern" leviathan, one which North Atlantic whalers may never have seen; frightening legends about the sperm whale are especially prevalent among the northerners. The stories concerning Moby Dick are especially fabulous. One rumor is that he is ubiquitous - that he can be in several places at once. Indeed, says Ishmael, this myth is not surprising, for the whale does seem capable of swimming at amazing speed. Another fable regarding Moby Dick is that he is immortal-how else could he have survived so many attacks?

Even if the fabulous reports are ignored, Ishmael tells us, Moby Dick is tremendously impressive. He is much larger than most sperm whales; he has a snow-white forehead, a high white hump on his back, and a deformed, scythe-like lower jaw. Most striking of all, he seems to possess an "unexampled, intelligent malignity" which terrifies many of the men who have battled him. Among others who have suffered because of this apparent maliciousness is Ahab, who, trying to kill Moby Dick with a mere knife, lost his leg. Ishmael suggests that Ahab developed his abiding hatred for the whale not immediately, but in long months of anguished brooding.

Comment

We finally receive enough specific details about Moby Dick to understand his tremendous power - and to gain respect for him. Even more important, Ishmael shows us why Ahab has reacted so violently to the whale, and he suggests (though we cannot be sure that the suggestions are literally true) that Ahab may be mad. Our suspicions that the crew has a symbolic significance are proven by Ishmael's reflection: "Such a crew, so officered, seemed especially picked or packed by some infernal fatality to help him [Ahab] to his monomaniac revenge."

CHAPTER XLII: THE WHITENESS OF THE WHALE

Ishmael tells us that, for him, Moby Dick's most appalling characteristic was his white coloration. He tries to explain why this should be so. First, he considers whiteness in general: it adds beauty to many natural objects (such as marble); it is often connected with royalty; it is frequently a symbol of joy; in several religions it is symbolic of the greatest purity and power-yet for all these good and noble connotations, there is still a vague "something" about whiteness that is frightening. Next Ishmael reflects on whiteness in animals: the polar bears and the white shark are specially terrifying; the albatross is linked to several superstitious fears; the albino horse, the "White Squall" of the Pacific, and the whiteness of the dead all have especially disturbing aspects. Why is all this so? Because whiteness itself is somehow frightening. The bravest of men, when shrouded in a white fog at sea, or surrounded by ice and snow in the Antarctic, will feel an unnamed fear grasp him. Do you think I'm letting my imagination get the best of me? asks Ishmael. How, then, do you explain the instinct by which a domesticated horse reacts in panic to the musky hide of a wild buffalo? (In other words, there are mysterious modes of understanding deep truths, modes which the rational faculties cannot comprehend.)

Comment

In this chapter Ishmael tries to explain the horror of whiteness - and fails, of course, because it is exactly what cannot be explained that is so disturbing about this characteristic of Moby Dick. Perhaps, he suggests, whiteness is so awful because "by its indefiniteness it shadows forth the heartless voids and immensities of the universe" (the great gap which Ahab finds behind Moby Dick's "pasteboard mask" and which Ishmael found in the serene summer sea at the end of Chapter XXXV).

Chapters XLI and XLII are two of the central chapters in the novel. As has been noted in Chapter XXXII, Melville is attempting to make the whale itself the central material of *Moby Dick*. These two chapters in their intense concentration on Moby Dick, keynote, respectively, the nature of the quest for Moby Dick and the symbolic and **metaphysical** significance of the White Whale as an object of Ishmael's (and the reader's) interest. They should be read and reread carefully.

CHAPTER XLIII: HARK!

One quiet night a group of seamen are passing buckets of water from the large storage barrel amid ship to the smaller barrel on the quarter-deck. One of them suddenly hisses to his neighbor, "Did you hear that noise, Cabaco?" The other scoffs at the idea, but the first sailor quietly insists that he heard a cough from a point below decks where no one should be quartered. Someone who has not yet been seen is aboard the Pequod, he feels.

Comment

Remember the "shadows' Ishmael thought he saw when boarding the ship.

CHAPTER XLIV: THE CHART

After the scene on the quarter-deck, Ahab went below to his cabin and took out his roll of yellowed old sea charts and slowly traced lines here and there. As he worked, the swinging lamp above his head threw shifting highlights and shadows on his wrinkled forehead, "till it almost seemed that while he himself was marking out lines and courses on the wrinkled charts, some invisible pencil was also tracing lines and courses upon the deeply marked chart of his forehead." Every night, Ishmael informs us, Ahab worked on his charts in this manner, trying to chart the courses on which he would be most likely to encounter Moby Dick. This might seem absurd, but Ahab knows the tides and currents of the oceans all over the world (he has piles of books on navigation in his cabin), and further, whales tend to swim in "veins" - long paths a few miles wide, which they follow by instinct. So despite various difficulties, Ahab's hopes of meeting Moby Dick somewhere in the South Pacific are not actually far-fetched. The results of Ahab's constant nightly concentration on his quest are shown, Ishmael tells us, in the fact that from time to time "a wild cry would be heard through the ship; and with glaring eyes Ahab would burst from his state room, as though escaping from a bed that was on fire."

Comment

Ahab's obsession with the whale is made even clearer by what he does in this chapter. But the images, as well as the action of the chapter, emphasize this obsession. The chart is very deliberately paralleled with Ahab's forehead in the second paragraph. The lines on the chart which the whale follows are like the lines which Ahab's quest has engraved on his forehead; the whale may be said to "swim" in Ahab's veins as it swims in the "veins" on the chart and in the ocean. But the whale in the ocean is a gigantic animal; the whale in the little world of Ahab's brain is a demon.

Note that this is the first clear use of the "flashback" technique in the book.

CHAPTER XLV: THE AFFIDAVIT

Ishmael decides to substantiate the comments he has made concerning the possibility of one man's encountering the same whale twice. He knows of three instances in which a man has killed a whale and found his own old harpoons imbedded in the whale's flesh. Further, sperm whales have often been recognizable to the whaling fleet at large, usually because of reputations for violence. "Rinaldo Rinaldi," "Timor Tom," and "New Zealand Jack" were such whales-whales that literally made names for themselves by their behavior. Ishmael also wants to prove that his descriptions of the terrifying powers of the whale are not exaggerated, but factual. He mentions first, that, although few outside the whaling industry know it, most whaleships lose one or more men per voyage. Second, says Ishmael, a sperm whale may actually be heavy and powerful enough to sink a ship! He cites examples of a whaler and a warship which were rammed by sperm whales: the former sank and the latter had to be repaired. Other instances of the whale's immense power are given, such as the case of the small sloop which was lifted out of the water on a whale's back, and several incidents in which full-sized ships were towed by harpooned sperm whales.

Comment

As in the "Extracts" and elsewhere, Ishmael piles up examples, some factual and some conjectural, from a wide variety of times and places. Note that Melville is again preparing us for further events, especially the **catastrophe** of the conclusion.

MOBY DICK

TEXTUAL ANALYSIS

CHAPTERS 46-63

CHAPTER XLVI: SURMISES

Ahab, though burning with the desire to meet Moby Dick, urges his crew to keep a sharp watch for whales. He has several reasons for doing this: he wants to keep the men in practice for his ultimate goal, Moby Dick; he must keep Starbuck busy to prevent him from rebelling against Ahab's quest; he wants to prevent "the full terror of the voyage" from engaging the men's superstitious imaginations; he wants to keep the crew's crude appetite for excitement well satisfied. Furthermore, he has announced a plan which amounts to stealing the Pequod from its rightful owners in order to use it for his own purposes; the crew, in this situation, has the right to mutiny. Therefore he will obscure the eventual aim of the voyage, as far as he can, by running the ship as if it were on an ordinary whaling cruise.

CHAPTER XLVII: THE MAT-MAKER

Ishmael and Queequeg are working together one hot, cloudy afternoon, weaving a mat of crude yarns. Ishmael muses on what he and Queequeg are doing: it is as if the two were "weaving away at the Fates," for the rigid strands (the warp) remind him of necessity, the loose strands which are interwoven (the woof) remind him of free will, and Queequeg's sword, used to tighten the strands together (acting as a shuttle) reminds him of chance. As he reflects upon how life is comprised of these three elements-necessity, free will, and chance-Ishmael is startled out of his daydreams by an unearthly cry from Tashtego, as the masthead: "There she blows!" A school of whales has been sighted, and a wild flurry of activity follows. The whaleboats are swung over the sides, and all hands are poised to swing into action as soon as the whales come to the surface after their dive. At this tense moment a shout is heard; all hands glance at Ahab, and, amazed, they see him surrounded by "five dusky phantoms that seemed fresh formed out of air."

Comment

The "five phantoms" who appear here are the "shadows" Ishmael saw through the mist at Nantucket - they are also the source of the mysterious cough of Chapter XLIII. Notice that Melville, calling them "shadows" and "phantoms," stresses their insubstantiality throughout the book.

Is the figure of the mat, woven by three forces, a good **metaphor** for life or reality?

CHAPTER XLVIII: THE FIRST LOWERING

The "phantoms" prove to be the crew for Ahab's own whaleboat. At Ahab's order, the three boats of the mates drop into the sea and pull away; Ahab's boat follows immediately. Starbuck whispers direct, earnest exhortations to his men; Stubb's commands are "compounded of fun and fury," and he uses a wild conglomeration of jargon and **imagery** in them; little Flask roars and dances, while insisting that his men beach the boat on the whale's back. The boats race furiously after the whales, and catch up to them just as a storm breaks. In Starbuck's boat (in which Ishmael is rowing) Queequeg darts his harpoon at a whale as wind and waves overturn the boat. The boat, though swamped, is unharmed, and the men spend a miserable night in it, rocking on a rough sea. At dawn the Pequod suddenly bears down on them out of the fog. They leap for their lives as the ship grinds over the whaleboat, and are picked up a few minutes later.

Comment

This chapter is Ishmael's introduction to the actualities of whaling. Besides being an intensely exciting "action" **episode**, it presents us with a view of the deadly dangers of whaling, and also conveys ominous suggestions for the future.

CHAPTER XLIX THE HYENA

There are times, Ishmael avers, when life seems a colossal practical joke. Such a time is likely to come at a moment of extreme peril, such as the crisis through which Ishmael has just passed during the first lowering. He asks Queequeg, Stubb, and Flask if the kind of danger he has just encountered is common in whaling, and he is assured by each in turn that it is very common indeed. Considering the various pitfalls awaiting him during the rest of the voyage - the general danger of whaling, the added dangers of storm and sea, and the very special danger involved in hunting Moby Dick-Ishmael decides that the most prudent thing to do is to go below and make out his will. Queequeg acts as witness for the will, as well as beneficiary.

Ishmael adds that it may seem odd to the reader that devil-may-care sailors should be fond of making wills, but such is the case. This will is the fourth that Ishmael has made.

Comment

Two factors should be noted in this chapter:

1. Ishmael's concluding remarks about whalemen and wills are intended to emphasize the fact that they face death on a daily basis.

2. The "hyena" referred to in the chapter's title is a reference to the universe as a "laughing hyena" - a scavenger that picks over the bones of dead carcasses and seems to laugh when nothing is funny.

CHAPTER L: AHAB'S BOAT AND CREW. FEDALLAH

Stubb and Flask discuss the remarkable fact that Ahab went out in a whaleboat. Stubb thinks Ahab's daring is wonderful, but the unimaginative Flask is not impressed: Ahab's leg is not off at the hip, but at the knee, so there is little to admire in his feat!

Ishmael tells us that it has often been argued among whalemen whether the captain himself should go out in a whaleboat. In Ahab's case the risk is intensified by his disability, and it is certain that the Pequod's owners would not want him to chase whales personally. Ahab therefore provided himself with his own boat crew, and took personal care in readying a boat for his own needs. The crew is odd, but no more peculiar than many a group that has assembled aboard a whaler, so they blend in with the rest of the Pequod's crew quickly enough-except for their leader, Fedallah. He remains a mystery, especially in that he seems to have some undefinable influence upon Ahab. Ishmael cannot say where he came from, but suggests that he is a type seen occasionally in the islands southeast of the Asian mainland.

Comment

Fedallah, as we see later in the novel (shockingly in the last chapter) is a Parsee - a descendant of a Persian religious sect known as Zoroastrians. The Zoroastrians believe that there are two basic principles, good and evil, constantly struggling in the world. Has this simplified view of the complexity of morality affected Ahab so as to convince him absolutely of the justice of his cause? Or is Fedallah, as will often be rather ambiguously hinted, a kind of Satanic figure who is trying to tempt Ahab to destruction?

CHAPTER LI: THE SPIRIT-SPOUT

The Pequod sails southward peacefully for weeks, with no further sight of whales. One serene moonlight night, however, the silence is broken by Fedallah's weird voice: "There she blows!" He has spied a silvery spout far ahead in the midnight sea from his perch on the mainmast. Although, as Ishmael tells us, "Not one whaleman in a hundred would venture a lowering" at night, Ahab gives chase with all sails crowded on the Pequod's masts. But the spout is seen no more that night. Several nights later the spout is seen again and pursued, with the same result. Thereafter the mysterious object is frequently seen, but the Pequod never gets near it. The superstitious seamen fear that the spout is Moby Dick's, perhaps luring them onward toward destruction.

Soon the ship reaches the Cape of Good Hope (notorious for terrible weather), and for days fights its way through savage wind and waves. Sea birds perch in swarms in the rigging, and strange forms swim in the water around the Pequod. Ishmael suggests that condemned souls may be animating the sea creatures which the ship encounters. During the passage around the Cape, Ahab spends a great deal of time on deck, both day and night, looking doggedly ahead in the teeth of the worst storms, facing toward his goal.

Comment

The description of the passage around Cape Horn is gripping, even though no real action takes place in this chapter. More important, however, are two other aspects:

1. The fact that a "spirit spout" which may be Moby Dick's leads the Pequod from serene seas into the savage weather of the Cape is suggestive of dangers ahead.

2. Ahab's furious determination is understood by his remaining on deck, seemingly endlessly, in such foul weather.

CHAPTER LII: THE ALBATROSS

As the Pequod heads toward the Indian Ocean after rounding Africa, it encounters another ship named the Goney, or Albatross. (The stranger's name seems appropriate, for, like the bird whose name it bears, it is a bleached and faded white, with salt spray caked all over it after a four-year whaling cruise.) The two ships pass so close to each other that their swaying mastheads almost touch, but no word is spoken by the lookouts. Down on the deck, Ahab calls to the Goney: "Ship ahoy! Have ye seen the White Whale?" As the other captain prepares to shout a reply, his speaking-trumpet slips from his hand into the sea, and his unaided voice cannot be heard over the rising wind as the ships move farther and farther apart. The seamen of the Pequod eye each other silently because of this ominous accident at the simple mention of Moby Dick to another ship. As the wakes of the two ships cross, a school of little fish that has been following the Pequod for several days races to the sides of the Goney. Ahab, peering down into the water, is heard to murmur sadly, "Swim away from me, do ye?"

Comment

Two points are of special note in this chapter:

1. The meeting with the Goney is the first of nine encounters between the Pequod and other ships. The meetings, some of them "gams" (to be explained in the next chapter), all imply some kind of warning for Ahab, and become increasingly ominous as time passes.

2. Ahab indicates in his reaction to the fish (and Melville seems to want to suggest that he's right) that he feels nature is against him in his quest for the White Whale.

CHAPTER LIII: THE GAM

Ishmael remarks that two strangers meeting in a wilderness will stop and chat with one another for a moment. Even more, then, should two whaleships meeting in the untold thousands of miles of the ocean stop for a brief visit with one another. Ishmael tells us that "of all ships sailing the sea, the whalers have most reason to be sociable - and they are so." Their social visits, called gams, consist of a meeting between the two captains on one boat and the two chief mates on the other, with an interchange of news and information about whaling, and perhaps the conveying of a letter or a package from one ship, if it should be outward bound, to the other which has been cruising for a longer period. One peculiarity about gamming is that the whaler officer must stand upright in a whaleboat, without anything to support himself with, while making the trip from one ship to the other.

Comment

Ahab, Ishmael, tells us, is never interested in a gam unless it appears likely to provide him with information about Moby Dick. He has left the land behind him in his zeal to kill the White whale; now he begins to ignore the society of the sea, too, if it has no bearing on his quest.

CHAPTER LIV: THE TOWN-HO'S STORY

Shortly after passing the Goney, Ishmael tells us, the Pequod had a gam with another whaler, the Town-Ho. Three of the Town-Ho's men told a fascinating story to Tashtego, who eventually told it to others of the Pequod's crew. Ahab, however, never heard the story. Ishmael tells it as he repeated it to two young men in Lima, Peru.

The Town-Ho, a Nantucket whaler cruising the Pacific, sprang a leak which, while not serious, required that her pumps be manned a couple of hours a day. The chief mate, an ugly man named Radney, hated Steelkilt, the handsome leader of one of the pumping gangs. One evening, out of sheer spite, Radney ordered the exhausted Steelkilt to do a menial job that was not his duty. When Steelkilt refused, the mate threatened him with a hammer, and when the hammer grazed Steelkilt's cheek, he crushed Radney's jaw with one terrific punch. The officers immediately tried to subdue Steelkilt, but he and several others fought their way up to the forecastle deck, set up a barricade, and refused to return to work until the captain promised that there would be no punishment. Their demand was refused, whereupon they voluntarily accepted imprisonment in the hold. Eventually they gave up one by one, until only Steelkilt and two others were left; then the last two betrayed the fact that Steelkilt planned to mutiny. The two were flogged, but because of something Steelkilt whispered, the captain decided not to whip him. However, the cowardly Radney stepped forward and, despite Steelkilt's threats, flogged him.

After this **episode** things appeared to return to normal, but actually Steelkilt was planning to murder Radney in the middle of some night watch. Just as Steelkilt was creeping up on Radney to smash his skull and heave him overboard, a cry came from the masthead that a gigantic whale was in sight. The boats dropped into the sea and gave chase to the whale-Moby Dick. Radney's boat harpooned the White Whale, but as the whaleboat approached, Moby Dick bumped it, spilling Radney into the sea. In a fury, the Whale seized Radney in his jaws and mangled him. The boats chased Moby Dick again, but could not catch him, so they returned to the ship. At the first harbor, Steelkilt and most of the others deserted the Town-Ho, and the captain was forced to recruit Tahitians for the rest of the voyage.

Comment

This is one of the most fascinating - and difficult - chapters in *Moby Dick*. Some critics see Steelkilt as a symbol of democracy, or Christianity, or both. Perhaps Radney is a symbol of pure maliciousness-certainly it seems that, in this instance, *Moby Dick* is an instrument of divine justice. Is Radney a "looming" for Ahab? (Recall that Ahab never hears this story, as he did not hear the reply of the Goney's captain.) Is this chapter a kind of capsulized summary of the entire novel? The whole chapter is shot through with ambiguous religious references-is there some kind of religious allegory hidden here?

Note that this chapter can stand alone as a story in itself, despite its relationship to the novel. It was, in fact, published separately in 1851.

CHAPTER LV: OF THE MONSTROUS PICTURES OF WHALES

Ishmael says that since he is soon going to give us a vivid and realistic portrait of the whale; he will first give us a view of some of the distorted pictures of him in the arts, sciences, and general life. The oldest of these fantastic representations are in Hindu, Egyptian, and Greek sculptures. (The oldest of all, representing the whale as half man, is in a cavern-pagoda in India.) But Guido's picture of the whale (early seventeenth-century Italian), Hogart's (eighteenth-century English), and others by other artists are hardly more accurate. (Note: again Melville is showing the widespread attractiveness of the whale, in many countries and many eras.) Among the pictures of whales produced by whalers and scientists, there are hardly any better representations: the flukes are vertical instead of horizontal, or the whale itself looks like a log, or a squash, or, in one case, "much like an amputated sow." And what of the popular pictures of whales on signs outside oil-dealers' shops? Worse yet. However, these mistakes are understandable, says Ishmael, for the only way one can really see the whale is while he is surging along in the ocean, and then most of him is out of sight. Only by going whaling can one get much of an idea of what leviathan truly is - and then the danger is so great that it might be better not to be too curious about the whale, after all.

Comment

Again, as in Chapter XXXII ("Cetology") we are teased with a major question, indirectly put: "What is the whale?" Ishmael (and the author) hints that "the truth" is not easily arrived at, and that only through dangerous encounters with reality can we discover that truth. (Recall what Ishmael has told us of the dangers of all "deep thinking" in Chapter XXIII.)

CHAPTER LVI: OF THE LESS ERRONEOUS PICTURES OF WHALES, AND THE TRUE PICTURES OF WHALING SCENES

After attacking grotesque portraits of the whale, Ishmael admits that there have been a few good reproductions of the whale's appearance. He knows of only four books on the sperm whale, of which Beale's is the best, especially for the pictures. But by far the finest portrayals of whales and whaling are two by one Garney and two by a man named Durand-both Frenchmen. They catch the whale himself fairly well, but better, they convey excellently the tremendous power of the whale and the intense excitement of the chase. By contrast, English and American works (though the product of better information) are mechanical and lifeless.

> Comment

To Ishmael, the most important facet of portraying the whale is to show its colossal power and vitality. The whale's essence seems, to him, to be pulsing, developing reality, not mere size.

> CHAPTER LVII: OF WHALES IN PAINT; IN TEETH; IN WOOD; IN SHEET-IRON; IN STONE; IN MOUNTAINS; IN STARS

Some of the best representations of whales, Ishmael assures us, are done by sailors who carve them with penknives out of wood, teeth, and other materials. Other replicas, perhaps not so faithful to the originals, can be seen on door-knockers and weather vanes. Startling resemblances are sometimes found in oddly shaped rocks, or the tops of mountainous ridges in distant countries. But the most striking "whale pictures" of all are the ones the man of imagination can see in the stars, constellation-like. Ishmael wishes he could ride the backs of such starry whales to examine the far heavens.

> Comment

Again, the ubiquity - the omnipresence-of the whale is suggested to us by Ishmael, as in Chapter XLI. This time, Ishmael even finds him in the sky. His intensely thoughtful bent makes us more and more aware that he is the ideal narrator for Melville's complicated "allegory," and also that his judgments are extremely important in organizing the story's meaning.

CHAPTER LVIII: BRIT

The Pequod sails through an immense patch of brit floating on the ocean. Brit is a tiny yellow stuff which looks like wheat; it is the primary food of the right whale. Numbers of these whales are seen swimming along (the Pequod is a sperm whaler), gathering quantities of brit in their open mouths.

Ishmael reflects upon the fact that landsmen regard sea creatures as generally repulsive, and the sea itself as an eternal mystery. The sea is the enemy, not only of man, but of its own creatures as well. It is a subtle, treacherous, "universal cannibal," "all whose creatures prey upon each other."

Comment

This view of the terrors of the sea should be compared to that presented at the end of "The Mast-Head" (Chapter XXXV). It should also be borne in mind when we read Fleece's "sermon" in Chapter LXIV. Is Ishmael suggesting that the whole world is really one savage, naturalistic battleground?

CHAPTER LIX: SQUID

Placidly the Pequod sails through and, finally, out of the fields of brit. The mysterious silvery spout is still seen from time to time at night. One beautiful morning Daggoo, the harpooner, sees a huge white mass rise once, twice, three times from the sea.

He cries out that Moby Dick is breaching in front of them, and Ahab quickly launches all four boats on the calm sea. The white mass slowly rises once more, and the men stare in awe at the immense, cream-colored blob in front of them. Flask calls from his boat to ask Starbuck what it is, and Starbuck announces shakily that this is the great white squid, a creature universally regarded as an ill omen among whalemen.

Ishmael tells us that the great squid is rarely seen, and that it is evidently a major source of food for the sperm whale. Apparently the squid clings to the bottom of the ocean, and the sperm whale tears it loose from the sea floor with its powerful jaws and teeth. Arms of the squid have sometimes been disgorged by sperm whales when they were being pursued by whaleboats.

Comment

Notice how skillfully Melville creates an ominous, unreal tone in the entire passage describing the occurrence itself, then breaks this tone with the relatively matter-of-fact discussion of the squid as food.

CHAPTER LX: THE LINE

Ishmael describes the whale-line to us, because he is going to refer to it more than once in the future. It is made of soft, golden Manila rope, two-thirds of an inch thick and 1,200 feet long, and will withstand a pull equal to almost three tons. It is coiled with extreme care into a tub about three feet in diameter and covered so as to resemble "a prodigious great wedding-cake" for the whales. The lower end is left loose, and has a large loop in it. Thus the line can be attached to a second one from another boat if the whale sounds (dives) too deep, or, if need be, the whale can simply carry off the loose line, rather than pulling the whaleboat under with it. At the other end of the line, two harpoons are attached by means of a rope called the short-warp.

Ishmael makes it clear why such care is employed in coiling the line. To give the rope some slack, it is passed back from the tub in the bow, around a "logger-head" (a short post) at the stern of the little whaleboat, and back up to the bow again. As it goes back, it rests on the oar handles on one side of the boat, just inside the oarsmen, and as it comes forward again, it rests on the oar handles on the other side. Thus the slightest kink might well mean the end of one or all in the boat.

Comment

Again, the dangers of whaling are stressed pointedly by Ishmael. Even more significant, he reflects that "all men live enveloped in whale-lines" - in one way or another, we are all at the mercy of fate, in imminent danger of death. Once again, whaling is Ishmael's **metaphor** for the whole experience of life.

CHAPTER LXI: STUBB KILLS A WHALE

Queequeg warns that the great squid (seen in Chapter LIX) is a sure sign of sperm whales in the vicinity. The next day Ishmael is standing mast-head watch, and, like everyone else on the Pequod on this sultry day, can hardly keep his eyes open. Suddenly a whale blows less than one hundred yards away, and all is commotion on the ship. The boats are quickly lowered, and the men paddle, rather than row, to avoid alarming the whale - but the whale becomes frightened, and suddenly a full-scale chase is under way. Stubb's boat closes in on the whale, and soon Tashtego harpoons it. The whale plows madly ahead, boiling up the sea and blowing furious jets out of his spout, pulling the tiny whaleboat along so fast that its stern rises completely out of the water. The crew pulls the boat up to the whale, and Stubb darts his lance into it time and again. Finally the great brute wallows in exhaustion, and Stubb probes deep with his lance, twisting it until he finds the whale's heart. In its death agony, the creature lashes about violently, blows horrible gore into the air, and then rolls lifeless on the sea.

CHAPTER LXII: THE DART

Ishmael wants to explain one point of procedure in the whaleboat. The boat leaves the ship with a whale-killer (a mate, on the Pequod) acting as steersman and the harpooner pulling the oar nearest the bow. In all the furious activity of racing after the whale, the harpooner is expected to shout and cheer on his fellow oarsmen, then, at the last minute, jump up and dart the heavy harpoon into the whale. Now, says Ishmael, this is a nonsensical practice. The success of the entire voyage depends upon how well those first darts are made - and yet the system is such that the harpooner is on the verge of nervous exhaustion when he has to throw the harpoon. Ishmael claims that the headsman should stay at the bow, do no rowing whatsoever, and make both the first dart and the subsequent ones.

Comment

Even here, Ishmael refers his reflections on whaling to the context of broader experience: "To insure the greatest efficiency in the dart, the harpooners of this world must start to their feet from out of idleness, and not from out of toil."

CHAPTER LXIII: THE CROTCH

The crotch is a stick about two feet long, with notches in it to hold the two harpoons attached to the whale line. The second harpoon is carried in hopes of darting it, too, into the whale, so that if one harpoon should pull out in the chase, the other will hold. Ishmael tells us that the second "iron" must be heaved out of the boat, whether into the whale or not, because it might otherwise be flung around and butcher the crew. The danger from the spare harpoons is multiplied when more than one whaleboat gets fast to a single whale. The harpoon is indeed "a dangling, sharp-edged terror" during the chase.

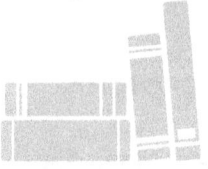

MOBY DICK

TEXTUAL ANALYSIS

CHAPTERS 64-81

CHAPTER LXIV: STUBB'S SUPPER

Since there is no wind, the Pequod cannot sail to the floating whale, so the three whale boats fix lines to the hulk and laboriously tow it back to the ship. The task takes several hours, and it is longer after dark when the whale is fastened to the Pequod's side for t e night. Stubb, who likes whale steak, exuberantly insists upon having a midnight supper from his victim, and starts to eat it standing at the capstan (a kind of winch used for pulling up the anchor). At the same time, hundreds of sharks nip at the whale's bulk under the water, tearing out neat blobs of flesh and awakening seamen by slapping their tails against the Pequod's hull below the waterline. Stubb, not hearing the sharks at first, complains that his steak is cooked too much.

MOBY DICK

> **Comment**

Ishmael pointedly compares the sharks' feasting on the whale to the sharks' banqueting on human bodies during a sea battle. Humans, he implies, butcher one another as savagely as the mindless sharks feed, by instinct, upon the whale. The analogy is intensified by the fact that Stubb wants his whale steak practically raw-he infers that the sharks know which way whale tastes best.

Stubb orders Fleece, the aged Negro cook, to preach to the sharks, whose noise begins to disturb him at his meal. Fleece damns the sharks, whereupon Stubb corrects him and tells him to preach a proper sermon. The cook begins: "Belubed fellow-critters" - and goes on to tell them that they must govern their sharkishness, for "all angel is not'ing more dan de shark well goberned." He suggests that the sharks with the biggest mouths should help those with small mouths to a meal, and Stubb responds, "Well done, old Fleece! ... that's Christianity," and tells Fleece to give the benediction. The cook's "benediction" is "Cussed fellow critters! Kick up de damndest row as ever you can; fill your dam' bellies 'til dey bust - and den die." After this, Stubb puts the old man through a series of minor humiliations, telling him that he doesn't know how to cook, making fun of his religious notions, and giving him special orders for meals the next day. Fleece finally departs, wishing the whale had eaten Stubb rather than the reverse and saying that Stubb is more sharkish than "Massa Shark hisself."

> **Comment**

This "sermon" by Fleece is the second of the book, and it contrasts markedly with Father Mapple's in many ways. The cook addresses the sharks as "fellow critters," and, in the context, we can hardly doubt that Melville - Ishmael wishes to imply again that sharks and men are brothers, "fellows." What are we to think of this sermon? It is true that men must govern the "shark" in them, but is all "angel" simply "shark well goberned"? (Are men as completely savage by nature as this statement implies?) Further, is Stubb (whose utter lack of insight has been made clear in Chapters XXIX and XXXIX) being blasphemous in mocking Fleece, and particularly is suggesting that the altruistic ideals of Christianity amount to acting as butcher for the less capable? Is Fleece's benediction Melvill's view of the cannibalism of the universe? (The sea has been called a "universal cannibal" in Chapter LVIII.)

CHAPTER LXV: THE WHALE AS A DISH

The whale, Ishmael tell us, has been regarded as a delicacy in many countries. Sixteenth century France and England enjoyed it, for instance. But these days only the Eskimos and such case-hardened whalemen as Stubb care for whale steak. The whale makes too large a dish, says Ishmael, and is too rich - and furthermore, many landlubbers have a horror of eating anything from the sea.

Comment

Ishmael adds another touch to the **theme** of cannibalism by pointing out that Stubb adds insult to injury by eating the whale by the light of a whale-oil lamp - the whale aids in consuming itself. (In "The Cassock," Chapter XCV, we shall see that the flensers, or blubber-cutters, wear a protective coat of whale's skin, and in the following chapter, "The Try Works," that the fires for melting down the fat are started with scraps of dried blubber. In these cases, too, the whale helps destroy itself. In

Chapter LXVI, the wounded sharks attack their own bodies. The world does seem to follow the principles of self-destructive cannibalism.)

CHAPTER LXVI: THE SHARK MASSACRE

Generally a whale captured late at night is lashed to the side of the ship until morning, since all the crew is needed to cut it to pieces. In the Pacific this method will not do, because the sharks will devour almost the entire carcass of a whale in the course of a night. Here in the Indian Ocean the sharks are not so numerous; nevertheless, to prevent severe damage to Stubb's whale, Queequeg and another crewman are suspended over the Pequod's side on a scaffold, and they slaughter a great many sharks with the whaling-spades. These are broad, razor-sharp blades on the ends of twenty-foot poles. The sharks are so voracious that they not only eat each other, but even tear at their own wounds in a horrifying carnage.

Comment

For the third chapter in a row, Ishmael stresses cannibalism and voracity in nature. The shark is so vicious that it is even dangerous after death-Queequeg almost loses his hand when he tries to shut the jaw of a dead shark hauled on deck for its skin.

CHAPTER LXVII: CUTTING IN

The whale is caught on a Saturday night; on Sunday the gigantic blocks and tackles for stripping blubber are hoisted up the mainmast and the process of peeling the blubber off the whale begins. A hole is cut in the whale's fatty side by the mates and a hook is inserted into the hole. The men heave mightily on the windlass attached to the stripping tackle, and the blubber is slowly peeled off in a long strip (called a "scarf"), much the way an orange is peeled continuously. The whale flops over and over in the water as this ribbon of blubber comes off. When the scarf has been hoisted as high as the blocks and tackles will carry it, a second hook is attached to it near the whale; then a harpooner hacks the piece off just above the new hook, and while the second scarf is peeled, the first is lowered into a place in the hold called the blubber-room and coiled up for storage.

CHAPTER LXVIII: THE BLANKET

Ishmael tells us that he has given a great deal of thought to the subject of the whale's skin, and has decided that the blubber is its skin, for no other layer can be peeled from the whale's carcass. The blubber ranges from eight to fifteen inches thick, and is of the consistency of beef. We may get some idea of the enormous size of the whale, says Ishmael, from the fact that three-quarters of the "skin" alone of a large whale boils down to enough oil to fill one hundred barrels (approximately ten tons in weight).

All this blubber keeps the whale (a warm-blooded animal, despite Ishmael's definition of a whale as a fish) warm in the icy waters of the polar oceans. The value of this warm outer covering suggests, according to Ishmael, "The rare virtue of thick walls, and the rare virtue of interior spaciousness" - and he recommends that men be "cool at the equator," a piece of advice he considers hard to follow.

> **Comment**

Ishmael's closing reflections, inspired by the whale, seem to apply ironically to "hot" Ahab, whose sense of being cramped and hemmed in by Moby Dick contrasts with the "spaciousness" of the whale.

> **CHAPTER LXIX: THE FUNERAL**

After the blubber has been stripped off the carcass, the head is severed from the body (as we see in the next chapter) and the great hulk is turned loose to float astern. For hours the whale remains in sight, and a grisly "funeral" is held by the sharks and carnivorous sea birds. The hulk, if it is sighted by another ship, is likely to be mistaken for uncharted rocks or shoals, with the possible result that for years mariners will avoid the area as a dangerous one.

> **Comment**

Ishmael's remark about the "horrible vulturism of earth" repeats yet another time the **theme** of universal cannibalism which seems so important to him.

> **CHAPTER LXX: THE SPHYNX**

The whale's head is valuable (for the spermaceti, which will be discussed in Chapter LXXVII), so it is secured to the side of the ship. Ishmael marvels at the skill shown by the mate who severs the immense head-one third of the huge whale's bulk-from a body which has no neck. The cutter must reach an invisible point on the spine, through many feet of flesh, often in a rolling sea which covers much of the whale's carcass.

After the whale's head has been secured, about noon, the Pequod's crew go below to dinner, and Ahab comes on deck alone. He stares over the side at the whale's head, and then begins to speak to it. He says that the whale has plumbed depths that must forever remain a mystery to men, and has seen paradoxes on the ocean which no man can understand (such as the fact that pirates may sail the seas unharmed while honest vessels are destroyed by raging seas). At this point a cry goes up: "Sail ho!" Ahab is somewhat cheered both by the thought of seeing a ship and by the fact that a breeze is blowing up.

Comment

Ahab's soliloquy hints that he sees nature as aimless chaos, destroying the good and smiling on the evildoer. It also stresses the tendency he has in common with Ishmael to find in nature a vast series of parallelisms and analogies.

CHAPTER LXXI: THE JEROBOAM'S STORY

The strange ship nears the Pequod, and proves to be the Jeroboam out of Nantucket. Its captain pulls near to the Pequod in a whale boat but refuses to come aboard, for his ship is suffering from an epidemic. Stubb recognizes one of the men in the captain's boat crew as a mad religious zealot who was described to him earlier by one of the Town-Ho's crew. This madman thinks he is the archangel Gabriel, and his prophecies have so terrified the

Jeroboam's ignorant and superstitious crew that he has free run of the ship despite his uselessness as a whaleman.

When Ahab asks the Jeroboam's captain, Mayhew, if he has seen the White Whale, Mayhew tells Ahab of the terrible death of his first mate, who was smashed out of the bow of a whaleboat by Moby Dick's tail. As he tells the story of the mate's death, the mad Gabriel interrupts him several times with wild shrieks and dire warnings to Ahab. At the end of the conversation, Ahab remembers that he has a letter aboard for one of the Jeroboam's crew. The letter, brought on deck, turns out to be for none other than the dead mate; nevertheless, Ahab sends it down to Captain Mayhew on the end of a cutting spade. But crazy Gabriel gets the letter, impales it on a knife, and throws it up onto the Pequod's deck at Ahab's feet after screeching "Nay, keep it thyself ... thou art soon going that way" (Macey's way). With this the boat's crew ship oars and row away.

Comment

This chapter embodies a very obvious reiteration of the prophet motif mentioned earlier (Chapters XIX, XXI, and others). Gabriel was the archangel who appeared to Mary to foretell the birth of Christ (see Luke i, 26-33); this "archangel's" prophecy is destructive rather than joyful - but Ahab ignores it. This is the second "warning" Ahab has ignored.

CHAPTER LXXII: THE MONKEY-ROPE

Ishmael tells us that the blubber hooks were fastened to the "scarfs" on this particular whale by Queequeg. Fastening the hooks is a hazardous job, even for the whaling industry, for the harpooner must walk the slippery back of the whale, which is submerged most of the time. To add to Queequeg's danger, circumstances demand that he stay on the whale during the entire "flensing" (stripping) operation. Aboard the Pequod, the practice is to attach the harpooneer who does this work to the man who pulls the oar immediately behind him-so Ishmael is linked to Queequeg by means of a line, called a monkey-rope. Ishmael feels that his bond with Queequeg reflects the interdependence of all men; no man can survive without the aid of others. Ishmael conceives of this situation "strongly and metaphysically" - as well he might, for several times he is almost pulled over the side. To add to Queequeg's problems the sharks continue to attack the whale, and Daggoo and Tashtego continue to butcher them with whaling-spades. Ishmael muses: Queequeg's situation is every man's; "those sharks, your foes; those spades, your friends; and what between sharks and spades you are in a sad pickle and peril, poor lad." When Queequeg returns exhausted to the deck, he is offered a cup of ginger. Stubb throws the ginger overboard and has whisky given to the harpooner to stimulate him.

Comment

Again Ishmael underscores the close bond which exists between Queequeg and himself, even going so far as to say, "we two, for the time, were wedded" (recall that Queequeg said in Chapter X that he and Ishmael were "married"). As usual, however, Ishmael conceives of his personal experience as analogous to a larger truth. The "hempen bond" which brings "dangerous liabilities" with it implies exactly what Ishmael has suggested earlier, in Chapter LX: "All men live enveloped in whale lines." Here in "The Monkey-Rope" he says that we live in "this whaling world," and the "unsounded ocean [we] gasp in, is Life." Ishmael is still trying to see the whole universe in this whaling voyage.

CHAPTER LXXIII: STUBB AND FLASK KILL A RIGHT WHALE; AND THEN HAVE A TALK OVER HIM

The Pequod enters fields of brit once more (see Chapter LVIII), indicating that right whales may be near, and Ahab announces that a right whale will be captured if possible. This comes as a surprise to all, since the right whale is (as Stubb puts it) a "lump of foul lard." A right whale is sighted, two boats are lowered, and after an exciting chase the whale is killed. Flask, in one whaleboat, explains to Stubb, in the other, that Fedallah has convinced Ahab that a ship with a sperm whale's head on the starboard side and a right whale's head on the port can never capsize. Stubb and Flask discuss Fedallah; Stubb asserts that Fedallah is the devil, and that he, Stubb, will heave him overboard if he gets the opportunity.

Comment

Two points of interest in this chapter should be remembered:

1. Fedallah's influence upon Ahab is becoming apparent. Stubb says that Fedallah is the devil, and Melville coyly mentions that the Parsee stands in Ahab's shadow, so as to cast none of his own. (The devil, of course, is supposed to have no shadow.)

2. Ishmael (or Melville too) remarks that sailing with two whale's heads dragging it down, the Pequod reminds him of a man who counterbalances Locke's head (Locke,

the great English empirical philosopher) with that of Kant (the great German idealist philosopher, radically opposed to Locke) in his view of the world. He is still paralleling his whaling experiences and his general theories of existence - and will continue to do so.

CHAPTER LXXIV: THE SPERM WHALE'S HEAD - CONTRASTED VIEW

Ishmael decides to contrast the heads of the Pequod's two whales for the reader's benefit. The sperm whale's head is the more symmetrical and shows more character; it has a "pervading dignity." The sperm whale's eye, about the size of a horse's eye, is at the back of the jaw and the ear is immediately behind that. The most remarkable feature of the whale's eyes is that, separated by the gigantic bulk of the head, they cannot possibly present a single, unified impression to the great brute's brain; there must be two impressions, one from each eye, delivered to the brain. (This fact, Ishmael thinks, could account for the great confusion shown by some whales when being attacked from more than one side.) The ear is even smaller than the eye, hardly large enough to insert the end of a quill of a pen into it.

If we look into the whale's mouth, we see a glossy white membrane covering the entire surface. The enormous jaw, about fifteen feet long, contains rows of long teeth which are terrible to see. (Sometimes a sulking whale lets his jaw hang straight down into the water, far below the surface - then, says Ishmael, the jaw is even more terrifying.) The jaw is usually hoisted on deck, to have the valuable teeth pulled out with a tackle on the mast; then the jaw itself is sawed into pieces.

CHAPTER LXXV: THE RIGHT WHALE'S HEAD-CONTRASTED VIEW

Ishmael crosses the Pequod's deck and looks at the right whale's head, then begins to discuss it. It has none of the elegance of the high-domed sperm whale's head; on the contrary, it looks rather like a gigantic, moccasin-toed shoe. It has spout-holes and a crusty, lumpy green mass (called a "crown") on top, and an enormous lower lip and jaw which give it a pouting appearance. Inside the mouth is a huge tongue, and a series of vertical slots-which resemble Venetian blinds-for straining out food as it cruises through the water.

Comment

Ishmael-Melville's whimsical humor is nowhere more apparent than in this chapter. His description of the "inglorious" right whale borders on the absurd more than once. Yet, even here, he is still grinding away at his more serious themes: the ladies who used whalebone in their corsets in the eighteenth century "moved about gaily, though in the jaws of the whale, as you might say" (see comment on Chapters III, XVI, LVIII and LXIV) and he again thinks of the whales' heads as suggestive of schools of philosophy.

CHAPTER LXXVI: THE BATTERING-RAM

Before leaving the sperm whale's head entirely, Ishmael wishes to point out that it rises vertically out of the water, and has, to all appearances, no sensitive parts whatsoever. The eyes and ears are twenty or more feet from the forehead, the "nose" (spout hole) is on top, and the long jaw is entirely below the head and well back of the great blank forehead. The forehead is incredibly tough - no harpoon or lance can pierce it. And all this dead mass which Ishmael compares in toughness to a horse's hoof - is driven by the most powerful living creature in the world.

Comment

In several of his remarks about the whale's destructive force and "battering-ram power," Ishmael is giving us perhaps the most obvious "loomings" we have encountered in the novel. He also, at the very end of the chapter, connects again knowing the whale with knowing "Truth."

CHAPTER LXXVII: THE GREAT HEIDELBURGH TUN

If we divide the sperm whale's head diagonally from lower front to upper rear, we will find the skull of the whale in the lower half and the "case," containing the precious spermaceti oil, in the upper. The case (or "Heidelburgh Tun," as Ishmael calls it, after a famous barrel in a castle in Heidelberg, Germany, which held nearly fifty thousand gallons) is as long as the whale's head-perhaps twenty-five feet - and generally holds about five hundred gallons. It is broken into from the decapitated end of the head.

CHAPTER LXXVIII: CISTERN AND BUCKETS

Tashtego, Stubb's harpooner, climbs the mainmast and goes out on the yard-arm (the horizontal spar on the mast) over the whale's head. There he rigs up a pulley and rope, with a bucket attached, for scooping the spermaceti out of the head.

Tashtego cuts into the case with extreme care, and the process of transferring the precious stuff begins. Toward the end of the job Tashtego, to the horror of all, slips and falls headfirst into the oozy case, now twenty feet deep! Worse yet, as Daggoo hurries to help him, the whale's head tears loose from one of the two giant hooks which have held it fast against the Pequod. The colossal head swings crazily over the sea for a moment, then slips free and sinks. Instantly Queequeg, with a sword in his hand, is over the side of the ship in an attempt to save Tashtego. Long moments pass, but then an arm is seen popping out of the water-it is Queequeg, and he has rescued the Indian.

Comment

Queequeg, in rescuing Tashtego here, extends what has loosely been called the "baptism motif" earlier. (See comment. Chapters XII and XIII). This is the second time he has saved a man from drowning, but it is not the last time. And despite his joking about. "Queequeg's obstetrics," Ishmael ponders this event seriously: Tashtego was almost "coffined, hearsed, and tombed" in the whale's head.

The language of Ishmael's humorous remarks should be noted carefully. Queequeg "delivers" Tashtego-he brings him back into life much as God delivered Jonah in Mapple's sermon- by causing him to somersault inside the whale's head-just as he flipped the bumpkin on the Nantucket packet-boat shortly before he saved him from drowning. Further, he delivers him from the whale's head "in the teeth ... of the most ... hopeless impediments" - suggesting the numerous images, scattered throughout the books which imply that all men walk into the whale's jaws, "all men live enveloped in whale-lines" (Chapter

LX), and so forth. Being caught by the all-swallowing "whale" of life or experience is the universal condition of men, and lucky is the man who has a friend like Queequeg to aid him.

CHAPTER LXXIX: THE PRAIRIE

Ishmael reflects upon the enormous wrinkled blank wall of the whale's forehead. Of all the impressive high foreheads-such as Shakespeare's mighty brow-known to man, the whale's is by far the largest, with the grandest wrinkles. Ishmael sees a "high and mighty god-like dignity" in the whale's forehead, as well as a vast mystery. To look at the whale's "face" is to see no expression or meaning whatsoever.

Comment

As Ahab did in "The Sphynx" (Chapter LXX), Ishmael tries to "read the riddle" of the whale's brow. But like the vast face of nature, the whale's forehead is inscrutable; whatever "mysteries" it may hide, Ishmael admits he cannot grasp them. (Note how this chapter reflects Ahab's conception that "reality" is hidden behind blank "pasteboard masks.")

CHAPTER LXXX: THE NUT

In a full-grown whale, Ishmael says, the skull will be at least twenty feet long. Regarded from the rear, the whale's skull looks like a human skull seen from the same angle. Toward the rear of the skull is a hollow of less than a cubic foot; in this recess the whale's brain is located. Considering the whale's bulk, the brain is small indeed by comparison - but Ishmael defends the whale by saying that its spinal column is as big around as its brain, and (punning on the word "backbone") that he judges a man's character by his backbone, not his brain. The whale's appearance is deceiving, says Ishmael - the whale, "like all things that are mighty, wears a false brow to the common world."

CHAPTER LXXXI: THE PEQUOD MEETS THE VIRGIN

As the Pequod sails onward it encounters a German vessel, the Jungfrau, or Virgin. Ishmael tells us that German ships are encountered rarely in the Pacific, although at one time Germans were among the leading whalers of the world. The Jungfrau's captain lowers a boat and hastens toward the Pequod, swinging in his hand an odd object which proves to be an oil can. Here is a whaler without oil enough to light a lantern! Aboard Ahab's ship he gets the can filled and departs quickly, but before he can get back to the Jungfrau, whales are sighted.

Boats are lowered from both ships, with the Jungfrau's well in the lead. Rowing mightily, the Pequod's boats pass all the others except that of the German captain, who thanklessly throws his oil can and other equipment at them. Infuriated, the crews redouble their efforts and close in on the other whaleboat. At the last moment, all three of the Pequod's harpooners dart their weapons over the head of the German captain; all three find the mark in the pitiful, maimed old whale that is their target. The old whale runs briefly, then he dives. For several ticklish minutes the three whaleboats stand almost perpendicular in the water under the strain of the great whale's weight, then the whale rises close to the boats. Dart after dart of the lances pierce the whale, which is discovered to be blind as well as crippled. Then Flask sees a horrible growth on its side, which he promptly stabs. The whale spouts blood in agony, and then rolls over and dies.

The three boats tow the hulk back to the ship, but after it is chained to the side it begins to sink, causing the Pequod to list alarmingly. Finally it becomes necessary to hack through one of the chains; the weight of the whale snaps the others, and the great corpse sinks like lead into the sea. Shortly thereafter, the Germans are seen ignorantly chasing finback whales, a species too fast to be captured.

Comment

The **theme** of cruelty in men and nature is underscored in two ways in this chapter:

1. By the unnecessary brutality of the mindless Flask.

2. By the condition of the whale that is killed. Ishmael says, "For all his old age, and his one arm, and his blind eyes he must die the death and be murdered, in order to light the gay bridals and other merrymakings of men. ..."

MOBY DICK

TEXTUAL ANALYSIS

CHAPTERS 82-101

CHAPTER LXXXII: THE HONOR AND GLORY OF WHALING

Ishmael tells us that he has become convinced that whaling is a very ancient activity, as well as an exalted one. The first whaleman was the Greek hero Perseus, who killed a sea monster to save Andromeda, a king's daughter. The skeleton of this monster, Ishmael contends, was preserved in a temple of Joppa - the city from which the second great whaleman, Jonah, began his voyage. A third great whaleman was St. George. His monster could hardly have been a mere "crawling reptile of the land," says Ishmael (stretching his defense of the whaling fraternity rather thin): "Any man may kill a snake, but only a Perseus, a St. George ... have the heart in them to march boldly up to a whale." A fourth whaleman of great renown was Hercules, who, like Jonah, was swallowed by a whale and then coughed up again. Fifth on Ishmael's list is Vishnoo, one of the three persons of the Hindu godhead: Vishnoo became incarnate in a whale. These five-Perseus, St. George, Jonah, Hercules, and Vishnoo - constitute a very special enrollment for the whaleman's club.

Comment

Note the similarity in technique between this chapter and Chapters XXXII, XLV, LV, and others in which lists are compiled.

CHAPTER LXXXIII: JONAH HISTORICALLY REGARDED

Ishmael mentions that some Nantucket whalemen doubt the truth of the story of Jonah and the whale. For various reasons they doubt that a man could survive in a whale's belly; further, one old man whom Ishmael calls Sag-Harbor cannot accept that the whale could have travelled from the Mediterranean Sea to Nineveh (where Jonah was delivered up) in only three days.

Comment

Ishmael's defense of the historical validity of the Jonah story is highly ambiguous. Melville is evidently voicing his own far-reaching religious skepticism through Ishmael in this chapter. Notice his ironic references to Biblical commentators, his sarcastic remark about "the highly enlightened Turks," and other little ironies throughout the chapter.

CHAPTER LXXXIV: PITCHPOLING

Shortly after the meeting with the Jungfrau, the Pequod raises a school of whales which flee from it rapidly. The boats pursue, and Stubb's boat gets fast to a whale. But the whale, instead of diving, continues to swim rapidly on the surface. Since the great strain this causes will inevitably wrench the harpoon out of the whale's flesh, Stubb resorts to pitchpoling to weaken the whale.

The pitchpole is a lance like the harpoon, but much longer and lighter; it is balanced in the hand and thrown in a long arc at the whale's vitals, then pulled back by means of the rope to which it is attached. Stubb flings the pitchpole into the whale again and again from the wildly careening boat, until the whale goes into his death-flurry.

CHAPTER LXXXV: THE FOUNTAIN

For thousands of years, says Ishmael, whales have been spouting in seas all over the world, but even yet no one knows exactly what the spout is. That the whale breathes through his spout is quite certain, but what about the nature of the spout itself? Is it air, or water, or both? Although many whalemen think the spout is poisonous, Ishmael doesn't; he hypothesizes that it is simply an acrid mist, which it is well to stay away from because it stings.

Comment

In this chapter Ishmael explains to us a fundamental principle which makes whaling more practicable - the fact that the whale, when it surfaces, instinctively breathes in enough air to supply it for about one hour's swimming under water. If its breathing is disturbed by whalers, it will sound, but will return to the surface shortly in an attempt to inhale the full quantity of air it needs. If the whaler can interrupt the spouting, he forces the whale to surface and become vulnerable to attack. The whaleman tries to time the whale.

This chapter also repeats notes which have already been sounded:

1. Ishmael suggests, because of the danger involved in approaching the spout, that "The wisest thing the investigator can do ... is to let the deadly spout alone." In Chapter LV he has already warned us specifically of the dangers of too much curiosity regarding whales.

2. The last two paragraphs connect whales and universal philosophical problems again.

3. Ishmael repeats the **theme** of determination again when he says that "the great necessities," not the whaleman's skill, conquer the whale that is killed.

CHAPTER LXXXVI: THE TAIL

Ishmael, parodying nature poets who sing the praises of animals, tells us that he will now praise the whale's tail. It is a thing of tremendous power and gracefulness, more than twenty feet broad in the full-grown sperm whale. Its colossal strength is increased, in Ishmael's opinion, by the fact that it is composed of three layers, with the fibers of the middle layer running crosswise to the fibers of the two outer ones. Ishmael argues that in the whale's tail, as in all things, "strength never impairs harmony or beauty." The whale does five things with its tail: swims by folding the tail under its body, then forcing it to the rear; swings the tail as a weapon against whaleboats; feels in the water for food - and for enemies - with the tail; plays with it by slapping it down on the water with a crack that can be heard for miles; and flips it high in the air when it is about to sound, or dive. The whale's tail, Ishmael implies, is almost as much a marvel and mystery as its head.

CHAPTER LXXXVIII: THE GRAND ARMADA

The Pequod sails through a passage in the Malay peninsula, called the Straits of Sunda, heading for the China Sea. On the way through the narrow straits the mast-head watches send up a cry; an enormous school of whales two or three miles wide is sighted. The Pequod crowds on all sails, and as it chases the "Grand Armada" of whales, a Malay pirate ship is sighted in the wake. The Pequod sails out of the straits into the Pacific, outdistancing the pirates, but getting no closer to the whales. The boats are lowered and the crews give chase until they are about to give up, when suddenly the school of whales stops, and begins to mill around in confusion.

The boats fan out and close in on the whales, each attacking a lone whale on the circumference of the pack. The whale that Queequeg harpoons drags Starbuck's boat (in which Ishmael is bow oarsman) into the very heart of the school, between the heaving bulks of countless whales. (The whalemen show an amazing bravado by shouting jovial commands to the whales as they scrape by.) Starbuck also strikes three other whales with harpoons that have druggs - big wooden buoys that will drag behind the stricken whales and tire them out-attached to them. In the center of this immense school of whales, all is calm, and Ishmael and the others get a fantastic view of the "ordinary" life of the whale. They see mothers nursing baby whales, and even one newborn whale calf still attached to the mother by the umbilical. Fathoms down, whales float calmly on their sides, eyeing Starbuck's boat. Others come up to the boat like pets, and Queequeg pats some on their foreheads. It is as if whales and men alike were entranced.

This astonishing scene is violently broken, however. Into the herd comes a severely wounded whale which has broken loose from a whaleboat and, by some freak accident, carried off a cutting-spade entangled in the harpoon line. In its agony this creature flails its tail about, hacking many other whales with the cutting-spade. This horrible event stirs the great herd, and hundreds of them begin to crowd into the center. Rowing and steering frantically, the boatmen scramble beside, between, and over dozen of whales, Queequeg prods gigantic sides with his harpoon, and oars scrape many a whale's back, as the boat barely makes good its escape.

Ishmael adds an **irony** to this hairbreadth adventure: the Pequod captures just one whale out of all these hundreds, or thousands, of leviathans.

CHAPTER LXXXVIII: SCHOOLS AND SCHOOLMASTERS

The immense school of whales encountered in the last chapter was rather unusual. Generally, Ishmael tells us, the schools are smaller, ranging from twenty to fifty in number. These smaller schools are of two kinds: one made up almost entirely of females; the other composed of energetic young males. The schools of females are always attended by one full-grown male, which acts as both husband and guardian to his harem. This whale vigorously drives away any other males which approach the herd - and, Ishmael points out, frequently bears the scars of violent combat with other bulls (males). The whaleman usually avoids these harem-keepers if other game is in sight, because they are inclined to be extremely pugnacious toward whaleboats. When they grow old they leave their harems and take up a solitary life.

The herds of young bulls ("forty-barrel-bulls," Ishmael calls them) are rollicking and reckless ("like a mob of young collegians"), and are more dangerous to encounter than most whales. (The most dangerous of all are "those wondrous grey-headed, grizzled whales, sometimes met, and these will fight you like grim fiends." Moby Dick is such a whale.)

CHAPTER LXXXIX: FAST-FISH AND LOOSE-FISH

Ishmael now explains an aspect of whaling he has not yet touched upon. Sometimes a whale that has been harpooned escapes from the boat that was fast to it, only to be recaptured and killed by another. What rules apply in such cases? Ishmael explains that the whalers have no formal code of laws, but that there are two universally accepted, unwritten laws for the industry: first, "A Fast-Fish belongs to the party fast to it"; second, "A Loose-Fish is fair game for anybody who can soonest catch it." Ishmael then adds ironically, "But what plays the mischief with this masterly code is the admirable brevity of it, which necessitates a vast volume of commentaries to expound it." (In other words, the simple, no-nonsense code of the whalemen-like all other simple views of a complex universe - is insufficient. Whalemen often resort to the law of violence - "hard words and harder fists" - to resolve their differences.) Ishmael ends his remarks upon whaling law by applying it to the rules of legal possession all over the world.

Comment

Ishmael's perpetual habit of seeing analogies between whaling and general experience takes an unusually bitter turn here. He implies that greedy kings, politicians, landlords, loan sharks, ecclesiastics, and even nations, apply the laws of fast-fish and loose-fish for their own selfish purposes. Rapaciousness is universal, even among men (think back to the **themes** of "universal cannibalism" and man's "sharkishness" mentioned earlier). On the other hand, all the abstractions that we seek-liberty, the power to influence others, religious belief, the whole world-all these are, in a way, loose-fish.

CHAPTER XC: HEADS OR TAILS

Ishmael extends the protest of the preceding chapter by giving an example of the injustice perpetuated upon the helpless by the powerful. A certain English law makes the whale a "royal fish," giving the King and Queen the absolute possession of any whale captured on the English coast. After much difficulty a group of English seamen captured and beached a big whale, which was immediately claimed by an official for a certain duke, who was granted his "right" to the whale by the King. Despite the logical, and desperate, pleas of the whalers, the official simply replied mechanically, over and over again. "It is his." A clergyman interceded for the seamen, but was told by the duke to mind his own business. Ishmael examines the logic of the law which gives all such whales to the royal family and finds it preposterous. Perhaps, he hints, there is a resemblance between the heads of kings and the heads of royal fish which makes the king's claim logical.

Comment

As in the reference to Lazarus and Dives in Chapter II, and in other parts of the novel, Ishmael shows his sympathies for the downtrodden here. And he uses the perennial defensive weapons of the "underdog," whether in literature or in real life - ridicule, **irony**, sarcasm, the lampoonist's devices.

CHAPTER XCI: THE PEQUOD MEETS THE ROSEBUD

Once more the Pequod settles into an uneventful routine, sailing over a calm sea. One quite day, however, an unpleasant odor warns the crew that the ship is approaching a dead whale on the sea. As the stench grows, a French whaler is sighted with a couple of blasted whales (whales that have died uncaptured on the sea) fastened to its sides. The practical-minded Stubb immediately suspects that one of the whales may contain a cache of precious ambergris (see the next chapter), and immediately begins to plot to get it. He approaches the foul-smelling ship, noticing that it is called the Bouton-de-Rose (Rosebud - another example of Melville's ironic humor), and asks if anyone has seen Moby Dick. One man aboard speaks English; he replies that he has never heard of such a thing as a white whale.

Stubb sees that the Rosebud's crew doesn't relish cutting up the two stinking whales, and he and the Englishman (who is first mate of the ship) combine to get the crew out of "this dirty scrape" of a job. While Stubb broadly insults the greenhorn French captain, the Englishman "translates" his words into a dire warning that the whales are diseased and will be the death of all aboard. The captain orders the whales cut loose, and Stubb graciously tows one of them away. When he is hidden from the Frenchman by the Pequod's hull, Stubb cuts into his whale and comes out with several handfuls of ambergris, worth, at the time, perhaps five dollars on ounce.

Comment

Of the many comic **episodes** in *Moby Dick*, this incident is perhaps the funniest. Even here, however (although much lightened by the humor of it all), we see a muted hint of Melville's **theme** of the predatoriness of man: Stubb takes ruthless advantage of the French captain's ignorance and the first mate's dishonesty to victimize them.

CHAPTER XVII: AMBERGRIS

Ambergris, we are told, is a yellow-gray, waxy substance found in sick whales; the name comes from two French words meaning gray amber (though amber and ambergris have nothing in common). It is valuable because of its marvelous odor, which is so potent that the ambergris can be used in making perfumes, cologne, and so forth.

Ishmael takes the opportunity, while discoursing on odors, to defend the whalemen against the charge that whaling is a smelly industry. It is only the northern whalers, who preserve the blubber whole and then boil in in port, that stink. The southern whalemen "try out" (boil down) the blubber aboard ship, while it is still fresh and sweet.

Comment

This chapter is noteworthy for its use of paradoxes (dear to Ishmael-Melville at all times). The sweetest of all substances, ambergris, is found in the midst of the most loathsome decay. It is named after a substance which bears almost no resemblance to it, and used by ladies who would be horrified by its original source. To describe the odor of the northern whalers, Ishmael uses the **metaphor** of excavating in a graveyard (death) for the foundation for a "Lying-in Hospital" (where life begins). Note also the nonsense etymology in this chapter - a device precious to Jonathan Swift and Washington Irving among others.

MOBY DICK

CHAPTER XCIII: THE CASTAWAY

Pip, the little Negro ship-keeper (one of the small complement which remains on the ship while the other seamen go out in the whaleboats), is chosen to replace an injured man in Stubb's crew. Pip is a bright and lighthearted person, Ishmael tells us (recall that he provided the music for the revelry in Chapter XL) - but not the hardiest of souls. On his second trip in the whaleboat, a harpooned whale gives the boat a mighty rap with his tail right under Pip's seat. The terrified Pip leaps from the boat and is caught in the whale line, while at the same moment the whale starts his run - the fouled line will strangle him in a matter of seconds. But Stubb orders the line cut; Pip is saved, the whale is lost. In a rage, Stubb tells Pip that if he jumps again he will be left behind.

Comment

Stubb's command that the line be cut to save Pip shows that he is not completely heartless. But at the same time, his anger and the fury of the other boatmen show how savage a business whaling is, and how savage the whalemen are. Ishmael comments ironically: "Stubb indirectly hinted, that though man loved his fellow-man, yet man is a money-making animal, which propensity too often interfered with his benevolence." This cruelty to Pip shows the other side of the devil-may-care bravado of such incidents as that in "The Grand Armada" - the whalemen are not merely brave; they hold human life cheap.

As fate will have it, Pip jumps again - and Stubb leaves him in the sea, thinking that one of the two following whaleboats will pick him up. But the other two boats, not seeing Pip, sight whales and chase them; Pip is left alone on the vast calm surface of the unfathomable ocean. Several hours later the Pequod itself, by sheer chance, rescues him, but by this time Pip has, it seems, lost his mind.

Comment

Nowhere is what Ishmael has called "the heartless immensity" of the sea more apparent than in this chapter. Pip's madness, Ishmael hints, is caused by the fact that the sea carried him "down alive to wondrous depths, where strange shapes of the unwarped primal world glided to and fro before his passive eyes." Compare this with the images of intrepid "deep diving" (Chapter XXIII), with the placid, yet terrifying sea of "The Mast-Head" (Chapter XXXV), and other **episodes** in which the sea is seen as an immense void, suggesting the vastness of life. Ishmael feels that Pip's madness may be a special kind of wisdom (mad wisdom is a well-known literary **convention**; compare King Lear's madness, for example). "Pip loved life, and all life's peaceable securities," Ishmael tells us; he hardly belonged in the hard world of the whaler. Is it especially suitable that, in this novel so full of paradoxes, it should be the most innocent and lighthearted who should have the most terrifying and enlightening experience?

Consider two other points:

1. Ishmael warns us pointedly that Pip's fate is a "living and ever accompanying prophecy" of the ship's fate.

2. The "law" Stubb gives to Pip concerning jumping from the boat is just as useful - or useless - as the unwritten "laws" of whaling seen in Chapter LXXXIX. Ishmael has said that we live in a "whaling world" - when should

a man jump from the boat? Compare Pip's fate with Ishmael's at the end of the novel to see how important the answer is!

CHAPTER XCIV: A SQUEEZE OF THE HAND

Stubb's whale is brought alongside the Pequod, and the long process of extracting the oil is begun. As the blubber is stripped off it is placed into large tubs; since it must be kept soft before going to the try-works (see Chapter XCVI), several men, including Ishmael, knead it continually. After the exertion of chasing the whales, this job, done under a tranquil sky, is so relaxing that Ishmael finds himself daydreaming. He imagines himself exhorting all his fellow workers to cherish the highest ideals of friendliness, and wishing he could always feel the contentment he experiences while "squeezing case."

Ishmael also describes several other parts of the whale which are worth mentioning while discussing the kneading of the spermaceti. Such unlikely items as white-horse, plum-pudding, slobgollion, gurry, and nippers are mentioned. Then he glances at the blubber-room, where two men are at work-one hooking pieces of blubber, the other chopping those pieces into chunks small enough to be carried. The chopping is done in bare feet and, Ishmael informs us, toes are scarce among experienced blubber-room workers.

Comment

In this chapter and several which follow, Ishmael fills us in on the actual details of the trying-out process, whereby the whale oil is produced. He nevertheless continues his "moralizing" and philosophical speculation.

CHAPTER XCV: THE CASSOCK

Before the pieces of blubber are boiled, they are cut into slices (so thin that they are called "Bible leaves") by a seaman whose title is "mincer." The mincer first garbs himself in the skin stripped from a conical section of the whale's anatomy. The skin is stripped off in one piece, turned inside out, and dried; then arm holes are cut into it. Thus dressed, he reminds Ishmael of a kind of priest or minister with a special ritual to perform.

CHAPTER XCVI: THE TRY-WORKS

The try-works are a large kiln made of bricks, about eight feet by ten and perhaps five-feet high, located between the foremast and mainmast. Two great metal pots are set into it, and under them are two furnaces. The top is covered by a hatch when the works are not in use, as is the front entrance to the furnaces. The try-works are first started on this voyage late in the evening, and are burning fiercely by midnight. Both the flames and the smell of the smoke remind Ishmael of hell as he watches, fascinated. (He is at the helm of the Pequod, guiding the ship in a fresh breeze.) The weird flickering of the fire and the red-lit shapes of the pagan harpooners laboring at the works, the sweaty faces of the night-watch and the wild laughter of the men as they spin yarns to each other seem infernal-even the ship itself, with a crew of pagans and savages, strikes Ishmael's imagination as "the material counterpart of her monomaniac commander's soul."

For hours he stands at the tiller (the jawbone of a whale), when, suddenly, he awakens from a brief doze and becomes "horribly conscious of something fatally wrong." To his amazement he realizes that the fire has, as it were, hypnotized him; he is facing over the stern of the ship. He recovers just in time, apparently to prevent the ship from capsizing.

Comment

This chapter presents one of the crucial messages of the book. Ishmael reflects: "Look not too long in the face of the fire, O man!" and goes on to say that "in the natural sun" all things appear differently-all lamps besides the sun are "liars." The hellish light of the try-works distorted reality. Yet Ishmael does not want to oversimplify matters and give a naive, rosy picture of life (recall his **irony** regarding all simplistic "rules" at other points in the story). The "glorious, golden sun" also exposes ugliness - "millions of miles of deserts and of griefs." The result of this painful truth is that "that mortal man who hath more of joy than sorrow in him, that mortal man cannot be true." Truth, then, makes men sorrowful - but too much sorrow is destructive, says Ishmael: "There is a wisdom that is woe, but there is a woe that is madness." Ishmael, then, seems to feel that man must place limits on his own urge to discover ultimate "Truth." But he nonetheless sympathizes with what Ahab stands for. (One wonders whether Melville really "believed" in the advice he puts in the mouth of Ishmael.)

CHAPTER XCVII: THE LAMP

Ishmael tells us that in a whaler, unlike a merchant ship, all is well illuminated below decks. On a merchantman oil is very scarce, but on a whaler, of course, it is superabundant.

CHAPTER XCVIII: STOWING DOWN AND CLEARING UP

After the oil has been boiled it is poured, still hot, into great six-barrel casks. The casks are wrestled about the deck, sometimes in a heavy sea, until they are sealed thoroughly. When the oil has cooled, the hatchways are opened and the casks are stored below decks. Then the whalemen clean the decks, using a lye made from the whale's ashes. A day or two after the trying-out of blubber, Ishmael says, no one could guess that a whale had been butchered on the deck of a whaler. But at any moment a cry may go up from the mast-heads, which will start the whole backbreaking cycle once more. Life is the same, in Ishmael's opinion: as soon as we think we have achieved something significant, another ideal presents itself, "and away we sail to fight some other world."

CHAPTER XCIX: THE DOUBLOON

Ahab has the habit of pacing the quarterdeck. One morning while stumping about the deck, he stops and stares at the doubloon which he fastened to the mainmast as reward for the first man to sight Moby Dick. The coin is from Equador; it has an inscription around its border; three mountain peaks and the sun above them with a flame coming from one, a tower on the second, and a crowing cock on the third; and over all are ranged the signs of the Zodiac. Ahab muses on the coin's meaning, and sees in the objects on the mountains symbols of his own indomitable self, and "stout stuff for woe to work on." Starbuck looks at the coin and sees the three mountains as the Trinity, and the sun as a symbol of benevolent righteousness.

Next Stubb looks at the coin and sees in it merely the cycle of the year and of life. He would spend it if he could. The mindless

Flask stares at the doubloon and sees only nine hundred and sixty cigars-what it would purchase. The old Manxman (mentioned in Chapter XL) sees there a forewarning of a meeting with the White Whale. Queequeg walks up to the doubloon and compares its markings to his own tattooings, and Fedallah bows to the gold piece as a talisman of some sort, for he is a fire-worshipper and the sun is engraved on the coin. Finally Pip gazes at the doubloon and repeats three times, "I look, you look, he looks; we look, ye look, they look." He then calls the coin the ship's navel, and brokenly predicts that Moby Dick will "nail" Ahab (another use by Melville of the prophet motif).

Comment

This coin, the reward for sighting Moby Dick, is as ambiguous as the White Whale himself. As each man sees, in a sense, his own soul reflected in the whale, so each of the observers reflects himself in what he sees in the doubloon. Some are subtle, some stupid, but all find something there. The most complex views are stated by Ahab ("this round gold is but the image of the rounder globe, which, like a magician's glass, to each and every man in turn but mirrors back his own mysterious self") and by Pip in his conjugation of "I look," which points out that each man sees what he wants to see. Ishmael clearly does not consider the speculation about the doubloon foolishness, for he says "Some certain significance lurks in all things, else all things are little worth, and the round world itself but an empty cipher."

Note the number of umbilical, navel, and birth images in the chapter. Can they be connected with other images-especially whaleline images, such as "all men ... are born with halters around their necks" in Chapter LX?

CHAPTER C: LEG AND ARM: THE PEQUOD, OF NANTUCKET, MEETS THE SAMUEL ENDERBY, OF LONDON

Continuing to cruise, the Pequod meets an English ship called the Samuel Enderby. Ahab hails it, asking if its captain has seen the White Whale; in response the captain holds up a white whalebone arm, calling, "See you this?" Ahab rushes over the side into his boat, and quickly pulls over to the Enderby, where he is hoisted onto the deck on a blubber hook. He and the other captain, whose name is Boomer, cross ivory limbs instead of shaking hands. Then Boomer tells the story of how Moby Dick took off his arm. The Enderby's boats attacked a small group of whales near "the Line" (the equator), and Boomer's boat harpooned one of them, which swam in wild circles. Suddenly a gigantic white whale breached near them (Ahab instantly hisses out his recognition of Moby Dick) and bit the line in half. But the line got caught in his teeth, so that when the whaleboat pulled up on the line, instead of hauling up on the harpooned whale, it bounced squarely down onto the hump of the infuriated Moby Dick. Boomer jumped into his mate's boat and harpooned Moby Dick, but the great whale smashed the little boat to pieces, scattering the men into the sea and forcing Boomer to cling to the harpoon he had just darted. Moby Dick dove, and the second harpoon tore into Boomer's arm, carrying him down - but luckily the harpoon ripped out, and the Englishman floated to the surface and was rescued.

Comment

This chapter is remarkable for its gripping presentation of Moby Dick's power. His significance to those who encounter him is demonstrated sharply in two ways:

1. The greeting of Ahab and Boomer: their special "handshake" shows them to be members of a select, though unenviable, "club" - those who have lost a limb to Moby Dick.

2. Boomer says frequently, "Thank the good God" that the harpoon tore out - that is, took only his arm, and not his life. Contrast this attitude with Ahab's reaction to Moby Dick!

The second half of the Enderby's story is told by the ship's surgeon, Dr. Bunger, an extraordinary person with a dry but zany sense of humor. With a great deal of incidental detail and digression, he tells that it became necessary to amputate Boomer's arm. His treatment of the affair is shot through with a kind of crack-brained **irony**. As he finishes his story, he notices that Ahab is burning with the desire to get after Moby Dick. When he jestingly offers to care for Ahab's fever, Ahab slams him against the bulkhead and roars over the side into his whaleboat. Despite Boomer's calls, the hot old man goes straight back to the Pequod.

Comment

We are told that Ahab "had been impatiently listening to this bye-play between the two Englishmen" - clearly, Melville does not allow Ahab to interrupt because he wants to present the reader with some of the best comic dialogue of the book. And, as usual, the comedy has serious functions:

1. Bunger's humor is rather sardonic. In other words he, as does Ishmael in "The Hyena" (Chapter XLIX), regards the universe as some grim comic joke. The whale's malice, he says, is not malice at all, but clumsiness.

2. And Boomer goes along with the joke. He cannot help the loss of his arm, and, like many men, jests about it to make the best of a bad situation. The one thing he can do, he says, is to avoid Moby Dick in the future. (Yet again, Ahab ignores an implicit warning he gets from a gam.)

Note how skillfully Melville uses the principle of contrast throughout this chapter, on several levels.

CHAPTER CI: THE DECANTER

Ishmael informs us that the English ship Samuel Enderby was named after the founder of the most famous whaling firm in England. This Enderby was the first man to equip a whaler to cruise in the South Pacific-in effect, he opened the greatest whaling ground of all. The ship named after him was a fine one, says Ishmael (he boarded it for a gam once, long after this voyage on the Pequod). The English whalers, following a tradition established by the Dutch a couple of centuries earlier, live very well indeed. Their ships are well stocked with solid food and good drink; indeed, when Ishmael gammed aboard the Enderby the entire crew got drunk and had to climb the masts, still "top-heavy," to take in sail when a squall blew up.

Comment

Besides rewarding us with further incidental details of the whaleman's life (and, for a change, pleasant details), this chapter furthers the contrast between the jolliness of some whalers and the fierce, austere determination Ahab inflicts upon the Pequod.

MOBY DICK

TEXTUAL ANALYSIS

CHAPTERS 102-118

CHAPTER CII: A BOWER IN THE ARCASIDES

Now, Ishmael tells us, he will introduce us to the mysteries of the whale's interior, especially his bones. How can he do this, when only Jonah has been inside a whale? Once, he says, he dissected a baby whale on the deck of the Pequod. Furthermore, as the guest of a South Seas island king he once saw the giant skeleton of a whale which was used as a temple by the natives. The bones were overgrown and entwined by the lush tropical vegetation (again Ishmael ponders images of life and death in connection with the whale) so as to form a shady bower. The natives had even built an altar with a flame which poured a jet of smoke out through the space where the spout-hole would be, and the jawbone was suspended so as to swing back and forth over the worshippers (the metaphor of being in the jaws of the whale is repeated once more). While Ishmael was measuring the skeleton, a group of natives angrily shouted, "Dars't thou measure our god! That's for us!" They then set about fighting among themselves, and Ishmael seized the opportunity to finish his measurements.

Comment

In depicting the quarrel of the natives over their own temple, is Ishmael (or Melville) reflecting his own religious skepticism, and mocking religious sects which quarrel among themselves? He has attacked un-religious zeal among the "religious" before, notably in Chapter LXXXIX.

CHAPTER CIII: MEASUREMENT OF THE WHALE'S SKELETON

Ishmael estimates roughly that the weight of a large full-grown sperm whale equals that of eleven hundred men. The skeleton which he measured on the island was seventy-two feet in length, which means that the whale itself was about ninety feet long. It had ten ribs on each side, ranging from five to eight feet long, a skull twenty feet in length, and forty vertebrae ranging in size from over three feet square to the size of a billiard ball. The ribs of a whale this size are so large that the natives use them as beams for bridges over small streams, and the skeleton itself reminds him of the partly finished frame of a large ship.

CHAPTER CIV: THE FOSSIL WHALE

Ishmael expounds humorously on the magnitude of the whale as a **theme**, and then discusses the fossil traces of the ancestors of present-day whales. He tells us that fossils or bones of whale-like creature have been found in France, Italy, England, Scotland, and the Gulf Coast states of the United States, including one complete whale's skeleton on a plantation in Alabama. When Ishmael contemplates how far back in time these remains go, he imagines himself transported back to prehistory, when there was little or no habitable land, and the whale was the king of the whole earth. Man seems a newcomer compared to the whale, who has been exploring the seas for untold ages.

Comment

Again Ishmael is seriously expanding his concept of the whale's age, geographical scope, and general significance, as in the "Extracts" and elsewhere. Why? First, because Ahab has taken it upon himself to destroy a force that has been a natural part of the universe since long before the existence of man. Second, because Ishmael really does consider the whale a mighty **theme**. His joking about writing with a gigantic quill out of a volcano sized inkstand in this chapter is really a serious joke. His thoughts about "Leviathan" really do, as he puts it, "include the whole circle of the sciences, and all the generations of whales, and men, and mastodons, past, present, and to come … throughout the whole universe."

CHAPTER CV: DOES THE WHALE'S MAGNITUDE DIMINISH? WILL HE PERISH?

Pondering the great age of the whale, Ishmael considers it logical to discuss whether his size has diminished over the ages, or whether the whale is liable to extinction. All the trustworthy evidence from fossils indicates that the whale of today is larger, not smaller, than his prehistoric counterpart. The ancient stories of whales measuring up to eight hundred feet are pure myth, as any whaleman can tell you. As far as the problem of the whale's being killed off is concerned, Ishmael has no fears. True, hundreds of thousands of buffalo have been slaughtered in recent years - but the whale lives deep in the sea, not on land. In the time forty whalemen kill forty leviathans, forty hunters can kill forty thousand buffalo. It is true that whales are sighted less frequently than in years gone by - but this is because the whales tend more and more to travel in gigantic schools like the "Grand Armada" rather than in great numbers of small pods. Finally it must be remembered that the whale can retreat to two absolutely impregnable fortresses - the north and south polar seas, where the ice floes will forever protect them from pursuit by whalers.

CHAPTER CVI: AHAB'S LEG

In his angry haste to depart from the Samuel Enderby, Ahab twisted and cracked his ivory leg, and he decides to have a new one made. Little wonder he should distrust the cracked limb, says Ishmael, for, although no one aboard the Pequod knew about it until long after the ship had put to sea, the reason for Ahab's hiding himself at the start of the voyage was a grievous wound he had received from another ivory leg. While ashore between trips, Ahab had been found unconscious one night, sorely hurt by the splintered ivory leg, which had broken mysteriously and almost pierced his body. Ahab will take no chances while hunting Moby Dick-he calls the carpenter and orders him to prepare another leg of whale's jawbone.

| Comment

We get a still further insight into Ahab's mania in this chapter, in discovering that he considers the misery inflicted by the splintered leg to be simply part of the grand general misery which he and all mankind partake of. There is something petty about joy, he feels, but woe is always grand and enduring. (Recall Ishmael's earlier comment in "The Try Works," Chapter XCVI: "There is a woe that is madness.")

| CHAPTER CVII: THE CARPENTER

The Pequod's carpenter, as all ship's carpenters must be, is a bit of a jack-of-all-trades: he paints decorations on oars, pierces ears, pulls teeth, and so forth. In a roundabout way, Ishmael paints an unflattering picture of him: "He was a pure manipulator; his brain, if he ever had one, must have early oozed along into the muscles of his fingers"; he is remarkable for "a certain impersonal stolidity." He considers human teeth bits of ivory, men's heads blocks, and men capstans. In short, he is almost a mindless, heartless machine, like Flask but much worse. He talks to himself, Ishmael says, "but only like an unreasoning wheel."

| Comment

Notice that Ishmael compares this impersonal mechanism of a carpenter to "the general stolidity discernible in the whole visible world."

CHAPTER CVIII: AHAB AND THE CARPENTER. THE DECK-FIRST NIGHT WATCH

The carpenter stands by his workbench, chattering to himself and sneezing as the dust from the dry bone that he is filing for Ahab's leg chokes him. He wishes that he had more time to turn out a better product (a purely impersonal wish; he has no feelings for Ahab's welfare in mind). Ahab approaches to see how the work is progressing, addressing the carpenter ironically as "manmaker." Then he falls into a reverie, in which he is ordering a "complete man after a desirable pattern" from the blacksmith-a giant fifty feet high with a brass head, much brain, no heart, and no eyes, only "a skylight on top of his head to illuminate inwards." Misunderstanding Ahab's muttering, the carpenter shines a lantern full in his face, startling the captain out of his daydream.

Ahab then talks to the carpenter for a few moments, telling him that he can still feel the sensations he once had through his own leg. He then toys with the stupid carpenter, talking to him cryptically about the possibility of his having a soul and other notions which are absolutely foreign to the lumpish workman. Ahab implies that he is a "pudding-head" and walks away in disgust, saying, "Here I am, proud as a Greek god, and yet standing debtor to this blockhead for a bone to stand on! Cursed be that mortal inter-indebtedness which will not do away with ledgers!" On his part, the carpenter can only wonder at Ahab, simply reflecting that Ahab is "queer, very queer."

Comment

For all his pride, we probably sympathize strongly with Ahab in this chapter. He is, at least, noble and intelligent. It is the clods of the world, like this carpenter and "King Post" Flask (recall that a king post is a block of wood), who cannot grasp the hurt and rage of a maddened Ahab, and who think that all is well.

CHAPTER CIX: AHAB AND STARBUCK IN THE CABIN

Twice a week, Ishmael says, the hold in which the oil casks are kept is flooded with a sea water to check the casks for leaks. If much oil is found in the water when it is pumped out, the seamen know that a serious leak has occurred somewhere, and the casks must be taken out and checked. One morning Starbuck comes into Ahab's cabin to report that a bad leak has broken out. Ahab is at his charts (a sure sign that he is aglow with the thought of Moby Dick), and, telling Starbuck that they will not stop to salvage the oil, he orders him out of the cabin. When the mate protests, Ahab sizes a loaded musket and shouts, "There is one God that is lord over the earth and one Captain that is lord over the Pequod-On deck!" Starbuck goes, but only after warning Ahab to beware-of himself. Later, Ahab appears on deck and orders that the sails be furled and the casks taken out of the hold for inspection.

Comment

This chapter presents an interesting, and almost crucial, clash of personalities. Ahab's obsession for Moby Dick is played off against Starbuck's godfearing devotion to duty. Ahab appears really to like Starbuck, but his reason for ordering the ship to a virtual stand-still is nevertheless ambiguous. Ishmael cannot tell us whether it is honesty or shrewdness (Ahab does not want an open break with Starbuck) that impels the old man to take this step.

CHAPTER CX: QUEEQUEG IN HIS COFFIN

Queequeg is among those who have to work in the slimy blackness of the hold, moving the oil casks to check for leaks. In the cold below decks he catches a chill which leads to a terrible fever, and in a few days he is on the verge of death. He makes an unusual request: he wants to be buried at sea in the kind of canoe-coffin which is supposed to be used for whalemen who die in Nantucket. Accordingly the carpenter is called; he takes measurements and quickly makes a serviceable coffin, which he callously carries forward to Queequeg for his inspection, despite protests from the crew. Queequeg, however, wants to try the coffin; he has himself lifted into it, and finds it suitable. After this **episode**, however, he amazes all by regaining his health rapidly. When asked the secret of his marvelous recovery, Queequeg simply says that he has some unfinished business ashore (he thinks that a man's death is subject to his own will, except for death caused by natural forces, such as whales). Thereafter, he spends much of his spare time carving on the coffin, especially transferring the tattooed designs on his own body onto the coffin.

Comment

Queequeg has already "resurrected" others; now, in effect, he raises himself from the dead. The coffin, of no use to him is nevertheless destined to play a most significant role in "resurrecting" another at the end of the novel.

CHAPTER CXI: THE PACIFIC

At long last the Pequod enters the Pacific Ocean, proper, as opposed to its Asian adjuncts. The Pacific is the greatest and most mysterious of all oceans, "whose gently awful stirrings seem to speak of some hidden soul beneath." (Recall the dangers of the tranquil sea as they are presented throughout the book-Chapter XXV, for example.) The placidity of this sea has no effect on Ahab, however; the closer he gets to his goal the more restless and feverish he becomes.

CHAPTER CXII: THE BLACKSMITH

Perth, the ship's old blacksmith, does not stow his movable forge in the hold again after helping to construct Ahab's leg. Since the weather is good, he stays on deck, doing all kinds of odd jobs for the seamen, such as repairing harpoons, lances and boat-hooks. Perth has a peculiar gait, as he shambles around the deck, which leads the crew to ask him many questions. Finally the wretched story of his life comes out: he was a healthy old man with a young wife and three children; the family was extraordinary happy until Perth started to drink. His business failed; he lost his house; his wife and children died; he was left alone in his age. Death seemed the only way out for Perth, but, like Ishmael, (recall Chapter I) he thought of the eternal mysteries of the sea and went whaling rather than become a suicide.

Comment

Perth's misery is presented as part of the vast unhappiness that is man's lot in life. In this general sense it parallels Ahab's wretchedness. But Melville seems to want the resemblance to appear even more forcibly: Perth, like the captain, married old to a young woman, had children, and, in effect, abandoned his family for a private vice of his own. Does Perth's misery forewarn us of disaster for Ahab? (Compare this chapter with "The Symphony," Chapter CXXXII.)

CHAPTER CXIII: THE FORGE

About noon, as Perth is hammering away at a pike-head on his anvil, Ahab approaches the forge. Seeing the sparks flying all about the blacksmith, he asks how it is that Perth is never scorched; Perth replies. "I am past scorching; not easily canst thou scorch a scar." (In other words, his sufferings have made him invulnerable to further sufferings-recall that Ishmael stressed his patience in the preceding chapter.) Ahab chides him for being too calm in his wretchedness, asking "How canst thou endure without going mad?" Next he offers to place his head on Perth's anvil if the blacksmith can hammer the furrows out of his brow - but Perth replies that those are the only wrinkles he cannot remove.

Ahab then gives Perth a bag of horseshoe nails, which are made of the strongest iron, and tells him to forge a harpoon head out of them. Perth forges the nails twelve rods, which Ahab welds into one piece. (While all this is going on, the fire-worshipping Parsee, Fedallah, walks past and bows to the fire.) After the head is ready, Ahab gives the blacksmith all his razors, ordering him to weld the razors onto the head for the point and barbs. Just as Perth is about to cool the whole thing in water, Ahab orders him to wait. He asks the pagan harpooners to give him enough of their blood to temper the weapon, and they agree; Ahab then pours blood onto the scorching harpoon head with the words, "Ego non baptizo te in nomine patris, sed in nomine diaboli!" After this, he selects a strong hickory pole for the shaft, and weaving the line into the socket of the head, forces the pole firmly into place. The diabolic weapon is complete.

Comment

In this chapter we see the second of three blasphemous rituals in *Moby Dick* (the first was in Chapter XXXVI; the last will be seen in Chapter CXIX). The demoniacal nature of Ahab's quest is being suggested ever more forcibly at this point in the book, especially by the last two rituals (note that all three have to do with harpoons). Noteworthy is the fact that, as Perth plunges the harpoon shank into the water, the steam burns Ahab's face, and he asks significantly, "Have I been forging my own branding iron, then?"

The importance of Ahab's blasphemous incantation is underscored (if it is not sufficiently clear immediately) by a letter which Melville wrote to Hawthorne on June 29, 1851. He concluded the letter by saying. "This is the book's motto (the secret one), Ego non baptiso te in nomine - but make out the rest yourself."

CHAPTER CXIV: THE GILDER

The Pequod is now cruising in the heart of the Japanese whaling grounds, and the whaleboats are busy many hours every day. The weather is beautiful, the sea calm: it is at times like these, says Ishmael, that, "beholding the tranquil beauty and brilliancy of the ocean's skin, one forgets the tiger heart that pants beneath it." The sea is like a vast rolling prairie (recall that, in Chapter LXXIX, the whale's forehead is called a "prairie," but a tiger heart may be found hidden in the whale), which puts the mind to gentle rest. Ishmael wishes that life were always this calm, but life and the soul are like the sea, passing through periods of calm to times of storm.

BRIGHT NOTES STUDY GUIDE

Comment

Among the many overtones suggested by this chapter, three are especially noteworthy:

1. Again Ishmael embodies the journey of life in the image of a sea voyage (and asks, "Where lies the final harbor?" What are we doing in this world?).

2. A "gilder" is one who covers something with gilt. The sea, Ishmael implies, hides its true self behind the golden appearance of these days.

3. Starbuck reacts to this gilding of the sea and its "teeth-tiered sharks" with faith ("I look deep down and do believe"); Stubb says simply that he is Stubb, and that he "has always been jolly" (he still thinks but infrequently); Ishmael considers the "tiger heart" beneath all this golden tranquility.

CHAPTER CXV: THE PEQUOD MEETS THE BACHELOR

A few weeks after the forging of Ahab's harpoon, the Pequod encounters another Nantucket ship, the Bachelor, which has filled its last oil cask and is now heading merrily for home. The Bachelor is decked out fantastically in celebration of her success: pennants stream here and there; the mast-head men have streamers in their hats; a whale's jaw hangs under the bowsprit; a barrel of oil is hung high on each mast. Music and dancing dominate the decks of this ship, whose luck has been astonishing. The Bachelor's captain invites Ahab aboard for a gam, but Ahab only replies. "Hast seen the White Whale?" The other's response is that he has not seen Moby Dick and, furthermore, doesn't believe he exists. Ahab tells the man to go his contended way; Ahab is "an empty ship, and outward bound."

CHAPTER CXVI: THE DYING WHALE

Some of the Bachelor's good fortune seems to rub off on the Pequod, for, on the day after the meeting with that ship, the Pequod manages to capture no fewer than four whales. One of the four is killed by Ahab, very late in the day. As the sun is setting, the whale is slowly dying on a placid sea. Ahab notices that the whale turns his head toward the sunset as he is expiring (Ishmael tells us that all sperm whales do so), and murmurs to himself, "He too worships fire." As soon as the whale dies, the body slowly turns in the other direction.

Comment

Ahab, ever ready to find deep meanings in what he sees around him, feels that the movement of the dead whale away from the sun is a symbol that the "dark Hindoo half of nature" is more powerful than the life-giving sun. He has committed himself to the forces of darkness: "Yet dost thou, darker half, rock me with a prouder, if a darker faith." (Compare Ahab's "darker faith" with the "golden" faith of Starbuck in Chapter CXIV.)

CHAPTER CXVII: THE WHALE WATCH

The four whales killed by the Pequod are widely scattered; only three of them can be brought to the ship before dark. Ahab and his crew keep watch over the other. Ahab awakens from an uneasy slumber to see Fedallah staring at him, and he tells the

Parsee that he has dreamed of a hearse again. Fedallah then tells him (as he has done in the past, obviously) that before Ahab dies he will see two hearses on the sea, "the first not made by mortal hands; and the visible wood of the last one must be grown in America." Further, Fedallah says that he himself must die before Ahab, to act as his pilot in another world. Finally Fedallah predicts that only hemp can kill Ahab. Ahab laughs unpleasantly, thinking that it will be a long time indeed before such an odd set of circumstances occurs on the sea.

Comment

Again the prophet motif is exploited by Melville - this time to make what amounts to the key prophecy of the book. Ironically, Ahab feels even more self-confident after these predictions, rather than being frightened by them. (Note, incidentally, the biting **irony** of this chapter's title - "The Whale Watch" seems to have nothing to do with the prophetic contents of the chapter, but in truth, waiting for these prophecies to come true does turn out to be a "whale watch," though not a watch over Ahab's dead whale.)

CHAPTER CXVIII: THE QUADRANT

The season for hunting along the equator approaches, and the crew waits day by day for Ahab to give the command to head for the equatorial line. Eventually, one glaring bright day in the Sea of Japan, Ahab comes on deck with his quadrant and looks through it very carefully at the sun, calculating his position precisely. (While he does so, Fedallah is kneeling on the deck behind him, bowing to the sun.) Then he addresses the sun as a "high and mighty Pilot," saying that it can tell him where he is, but not where to find his objective, Moby Dick. In a towering rage because the quadrant's information is so meaningless to him, Ahab dashes it to the deck and crushes it, shouting "Cursed be all things that cast man's eyes aloft to that heaven, whose live vividness but scorches him!" He roars out an order to change course. (From now on the Pequod will steer by what is called dead reckoning-using only the compass and estimates of speed rather than any astronomical calculations.) Starbuck asks Stubb what the result of such behavior can possibly be, and Stubb replies that he has overheard Ahab mutter that he must play the hand of cards which fate has dealt him.

Comment

Much earlier, Ahab threw away his pipe (Chapter XXX). Now he smashes the quadrant; the other navigational equipment will malfunction shortly. Ahab, more and more obsessed by Moby Dick, is leaving his human and geographical position in the actual world behind him "locating" himself only in terms of his relationship to the whale.

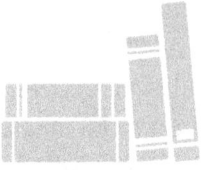

MOBY DICK

TEXTUAL ANALYSIS

CHAPTERS 119-135

CHAPTER CXIX: THE CANDLES

In the evening of the day on which Ahab smashes the quadrant, a typhoon (the most violent of all the world's storms) suddenly strikes the Pequod, tearing off several of her sails and rolling huge waves onto her deck. One wave smashes Ahab's whaleboat. Stubb, as usual, makes a joke of danger, and sings a rollicking song, but Starbuck warns him that there are omens all around them. The typhoon is from the east, where Ahab is heading for Moby Dick, and Ahab's whaleboat has been crushed at exactly the spot where Ahab stands when hunting.

As Starbuck is speaking to Stubb, the captain approaches in a flash shouts to attract the crew's attention, then seizes the lightning rod links, which should be hung over the side into the sea. At this very moment, the tops of the Pequod's three masts are lit up by corposants (a light caused by atmospheric electricity, sometimes seen on mastheads, church towers, and other tall objects), and many of the crew are terrified by the eerie glow. Stubb loses all his bravado for a moment, but regains it as soon as the corposants fade out. The light reappears, however, and once more Stubb cries out, "the corposants have mercy on us all!" Ahab's response is completely different. He shouts to attract the crew's attention, then seizes the lightning rod links and, with his foot upon the back of the kneeling Fedallah, says he is feeling the pulse of the lightning. (In effect, Ahab is challenging the lightning, or nature, to destroy him if it can.) Then he makes a tremendous speech of defiance, asserting his unconquerable individuality in the face of the power of nature. Lightning flashes about the ship, and he speaks directly to it, calling it his ancestor. Suddenly the tip of his "consecrated" harpoon, which is still in the smashed whaleboat, bursts into the same kind of flame that is playing over the mastheads. Starbuck shouts that this is a sign that God is against Ahab, and asks to be allowed to give orders to turn the ship around, away from this terrifying quest. The men spring to their posts, but Ahab picks up the fiery harpoon and says he will kill the first man who touches a rope. Horrified by Ahab, but even more by the flaming harpoon, the men scramble away from him.

Comment

This chapter, probably the most dramatic of the book, is marvelously theatrical. Melville is using all nature as stage props. Tremendous fire, blackness, storm, and battering sea-all are present, as are high emotion, conflicting beliefs, and clash of personalities. Ahab's speech brings his hatred for the forces that "task" him and "heap" him (see Chapter XXXVI) to a **climax**, and overwhelms the reader with Ahab's inflexible fanaticism of purpose. It also inspires a respect, almost an admiration, for his raging pride.

CHAPTER CXX: THE DECK TOWARDS THE END OF THE FIRST NIGHT WATCH

As the storm continues, Starbuck addresses Ahab, who is standing by the helm. He wants permission to furl a sail, but Ahab refuses-he wants all left as it is. He merely orders that everything movable be lashed down. Only cowards take down sails, he says, or back down on their purposes, in bad weather.

Comment

Ahab steadfastly continues to battle nature. He even mocks it, suggesting that the fury of the storm is nothing majestic, but a kind of gassy stomach ache.

CHAPTER CXXI: MIDNIGHT - THE FORECASTLE BULWARKS

Stubb and Flask are arguing with each other as they lash down the anchors. Flask points out that Stubb has said that there were special dangers in sailing with Ahab, but Stubb claims to have changed his mind. Specifically, Stubb says that Ahab was in no more danger while holding the lightning rod links than any man would be standing near a mast on any ship in a storm. (In other words, in Stubb's opinion Ahab's titanic challenge to nature was not so very bold after all.

Comment

Compare Stubb's reaction to the storm with that of Ahab and Starbuck in the preceding chapter, and with Tashtego's, in the following one.

CHAPTER CXXII: MIDNIGHT ALOFT - THUNDER AND LIGHTNING

Tashtego is high on the mainmast, lashing down a sail. He imitates the rumble of the thunder, and says, "We don't want thunder: we want rum; give us a glass of rum."

Comment

Recall that Tashtego makes only two other speeches in the entire novel (Chapter XXXIX), and one of these is about thunder at midnight. Tashtego represents a third possible reaction to the storm (and, by implication, the stormy forces of life) - unimaginative indifference.

CHAPTER CXXIII: THE MUSKET

Toward morning the typhoon eases off enough so that Starbuck and Stubbs can cut down the shreds of sail and replace them with new canvas. The wind seems to swing around so that the Pequod can now pursue her eastward course again. This "fair wind" cheers the crew, but not Starbuck, who sees it only as a wind which will take Ahab nearer to his mad goal. Starbuck goes to report the change of wind to the captain, and stops next to the weapons rack. He picks up the very musket with which Ahab once threatened to kill him, and for agonizing moments debates whether he should kill Ahab or not. He is sure Ahab's quest is morally evil, and equally certain that the Pequod's entire crew may die because of the reckless way Ahab is sailing the ship. He feels that he may be doing God's justice if he kills the old man, and there seems no other way to end the hunt for Moby Dick (for to hold such a mad titan as Ahab as a prisoner would be impossible). Finally he puts the musket back on the rack, and rushes on deck to tell Stubb to report the change to Ahab.

Comment

We have here the action of a good man - "Thou shalt not kill." But we also see Melville presenting another aspect of the great paradoxes of life. Ahab has, in effect, been asked, "Must man calmly accept the harm life does to him?" and his answer is a roaring "No!" To Starbuck the question is presented: "Must the innocent stand quietly by and let the evil destroy them?" His answer, apparently, is "yes." Would Ahab accept the restrictions of Starbuck's firm moral code? How can the innocent protect themselves in a world of sharks without adopting evil methods themselves?

CHAPTER CXXIV: THE NEEDLE

The following morning the Pequod is bowling along briskly on the waning winds of the storm. Ahab notices the sun rising in his wake, and rushes to the helmsman to ask what course is being followed. The man replies "East-sou-east, sir," and Ahab, in a rage, knocks him down. (The sun, of course, rises in the east; it should be rising over the ship's bow.) Ahab checks the compass, and to his consternation sees that the course does read east-south-east. The storm has demagnetized the compass needles and reversed them exactly. Before the fact can be spread about and perhaps frighten the superstitious crew, Ahab gives orders to turn the ship about. Then, calling the crew together, he prepares another needle for the compass, acting with the air of a sorcerer (the process is a very simple one, but Ahab plays on the ignorance and superstition of the crew, as he has done before). He calls himself "lord of the level loadstone."

Comment

Many of Ahab's experiences have seemed to be omens-several of the gams, for instance, and the accidents in Chapter CXIX. Here, nature appears deliberately to turn Ahab away from his pursuit of Moby Dick. But again, as heretofore, he ignores all warnings.

CHAPTER CXXV: THE LOG AND LINE

The Pequod's log and line, a device for measuring the ship's speed, has never been used on this voyage. But one morning, recalling his oath to steer by dead reckoning and the log and line (Chapter CXVIII), Ahab orders the log cast over the ship's stern. The old Manxman fears that the rope, rotted by salt spray and disuse, will break, but Ahab says it will hold. The log is heaved, and almost immediately the rope snaps. Ahab tells the seamen to mend the rope and have the carpenter make another log.

As the Manxman and his helper work to reel in the line, Pip gets in their way; the commotion he causes attracts Ahab's attention. Ahab questions Pip, and, as he talks to him, sees a reflection of his own sufferings in the harmless boy. Touched by pity, he decides that henceforth Pip will live with him in his own cabin. He says, "See the omniscient gods oblivious of suffering man; and man, though idiotic, and knowing not what he does, yet, full of the sweet things of love and gratitude."

Comment

The breaking of the log and line is still another warning for Ahab - and still he pays no heed. He walks away unmoved, while the Manxman says, "to him nothing's happened; but to me, the skewer seems loosening in the middle of the world." One thing does move Ahab, however-Pip's suffering. As we have seen infrequently, Ahab does have "his humanities."

CHAPTER CXXVI: THE LIFE-BUOY

One night just before dawn, as the ship is sailing into the equatorial cruising grounds, weird cries are heard for a time near the Pequod. When Ahab awakens, Flask tells him of these cries, which sounded like drowning men. Ahab explains that seals looking for their young must have made the noises, but the crew nevertheless feels uneasy. Shortly after dawn, a mast-head watch falls with a cry into the sea, and, although the lifebuoy is thrown overboard, the seaman never rises to grasp it. The dried lifebuoy itself, in fact, soaks up water and sinks into the ocean. The sailors feel more relief than pity at the drowning of the seaman, for they feel that the omen of the terrible cries has now been fulfilled.

Starbuck searches the ship for a substitute for the lifebuoy, but finds nothing suitable, so Queequeg hints that his coffin would suffice. After a brief discussion, Starbuck decides that the idea is a good one, and orders the carpenter to seal the coffin tightly and hang it in the place of the buoy. The carpenter (like the dehumanized machine that he is) is annoyed at the idea of having to re-fit a piece of work he has already done, but he obeys orders. (He is also irritated that Queequeg didn't die, because he feels that he did his work for nothing.)

| Comment

For reasons which will be clear in the final chapter, it is especially fitting that it should be Queequeg's coffin, at Queequeg's suggestion, that is made into a lifebuoy.

| CHAPTER CXXVII: THE DECK

As the carpenter sets to work to caulk the coffin, Ahab comes up on deck and begins to talk to him. He accuses the man of being a scamp for milking legs one day and coffins the next (in effect, of meddling with both life and death). To do this, he says, is to be "as unprincipled as the gods." The carpenter responds, "I do not mean anything, sir. I do as I do," to which Ahab retorts, "The gods again." A moment later the man says, "Faith, sir ..." and Ahab asks him what faith is. The carpenter can only respond that "faith" is an exclamation. (In other words, again the man "does not mean anything.") Ahab suddenly snaps at the man and tells him to get his work done in a harry, and, musing on the meaning of the coffin-lifebuoy, goes off to see Pip.

| Comment

Ahab is nasty to the carpenter for two reasons:

1. He already despises him as a stupid blockhead who cannot feel or understand what Ahab-or Pip-can. The soul of this lump can never be stung by life's injustices.

2. The fact that the man "does as he does," without meaning anything (remember that Ahab sees meanings in

everything) reminds him of the blind, feelingless forces which he thinks have buffeted and maimed him.

CHAPTER CXXVIII: THE PEQUOD MEETS THE RACHEL

The next day the Pequod sights a large ship, the Rachel, from Nantucket. Her masts are full of lookouts, and as she sails up close to Ahab's ship, she cuts off the wind, causing the Pequod's sails to slacken with a clap. The Manxman mumbles, "she brings bad news." Ahab asks her captain if he has seen the White Whale, and the other tells him that he has, only yesterday. The man, Captain Gardiner, boards the Pequod and tells that he has lost a boat, which was towed out of sight by Moby Dick. He begs Ahab to help him search for the boat, for his twelve-year old son was in it. He conjures Ahab by the love he has for his own son, back home in Nantucket, to assist him, but Ahab refuses, tells him to leave the ship, and goes below to his cabin. The stunned Gardiner leaves the Pequod and returns to the Rachel. Soon the two ships are far apart, but as long as the Rachel is in sight he can be seen tacking here and there, looking for survivors.

Comment

In this chapter we see one more example of the lengths to which Ahab's fanaticism will lead him. Not even the realization that his own son could have been in the other boy's place moves him. His cruelty is heightened by contrast with Stubb, who never takes anything seriously. Stubb remarks that one of the missing whalemen must have had some of Gardiner's property to cause the captain such anxiety. But when he hears that the man's son is missing, even the callow Stubb changes his attitude and he murmurs sincerely, "We must save that boy." But Ahab is not Stubb.

CHAPTER CXXIX: THE CABIN

As Ahab starts out of his cabin to go up on deck, Pip takes his hand to go with him. Ahab tells him to stay behind, however, for he fears that his pity for the Negro boy may sway him from his purpose. When Pip promises devotion to him, Ahab is deeply moved. Pip begins to weep for Ahab, who snaps out, "Weep so, and I will murder thee! Have a care, for Ahab too is mad!" The two clasp hands for a moment, and Ahab goes out, leaving Pip to talk brokenly to himself.

CHAPTER CXXX: THE HAT

Now that Ahab has met a ship which has seen Moby Dick only a day past, he is more on fire with his purpose than ever. His piercing eye seems to be everywhere, so domineering the entire crew that they do their job in machinelike solemnity. As Ahab's eye awes the crew, so the Parsee's eye seems to attract Ahab. The two are always on deck; Ahab even eats his two meals a day on the quarter deck (the Parsee, we are told, has never been seen to go below decks). Each day at dawn Ahab calls out, "Man the mast-heads!" and the long watch begins, ending only well after sunset. After four days, however, Ahab suspects that no one but the three pagan harpooners really wants to sight Moby Dick, so he rigs a special line and has himself raised to the main mast-head. Ironically, the man he chooses to see that his line remains secure is Starbuck - the one man of the entire crew who has opposed him and the one he would trust least to sing out if Moby Dick were sighted. (The God-fearing Starbuck, most respectful of human life, is most to be trusted with this task.) Before Ahab is atop the mainmast ten minutes, a low-flying sea-hawk picks his hat off his head and flies off with it into the distance.

Comment

In "The Monkey-Rope" (Chapter LXXII) we saw two loving "brothers," Ishmael and Queequeg, linked together by a rope that meant life and death to them. Now we see much the same relationship between two men whose aims are radically opposed - but we know that Starbuck can be trusted with Ahab's life, however much he hates his purpose.

The sea-hawk is almost nature's last direct warning to Ahab. One more such warning will be seen - the sharks in Chapter CXXXV.

CHAPTER CXXXI: THE PEQUOD MEETS THE DELIGHT

The Pequod sails steadily onward in its intense search for Moby Dick, and after another few days crosses a ship which Ishmael says is "Most miserably misnamed the Delight." Ahab asks his question, "Hast seen the White Whale?" and in answer the Delight's captain points to a splintered whaleboat. When the stranger tells Ahab no harpoon ever forged will kill Moby Dick, Ahab holds up his diabolic harpoon and, in a fury, shouts to the other captain that he holds the needed weapon in his hand. The Delight's captain simply responds, "God keep thee, old man," and turns to reading the divine service over the body of a whaleman - the only body recovered of a crew of five-killed by Moby Dick one day earlier. The Pequod does not move out of hearing fast enough to avoid hearing the sound of the body as it splashes into the water. The Delight's crewmen see the coffin (the new lifebuoy) hanging over the Pequod's stern as the ships sail apart.

Comment

The Delight is the last ship the Pequod meets on its voyage - and this last, sternest warning, like all the others, goes unheeded by Ahab.

CHAPTER CXXXII: THE SYMPHONY

A gloriously beautiful day dawns, and Ahab crosses the deck and leans over the Pequod's side. As he stares down into the sea a tear falls into the water. Seeing Ahab's pensiveness, Starbuck comes and stands nearby. Ahab turns, sees him, and addresses him. He begins to talk of his forty long years on the sea, forty years of toil and privation. He talks of the young wife he loves, and calls himself a fool for spending his life in such a violent trade as whaling. He tells Starbuck that he must stay aboard the Pequod when Ahab lowers for Moby Dick.

Starbuck's response is to urge Ahab once more to give up the quest and return home to his wife and child, as Starbuck wishes to return to his own family. The two speak excitedly of home and family for a moment, but then Ahab bows his head and mutters to himself, "What is it, what nameless, inscrutable, unearthly thing is it . . commands me; that against all natural lovings and longings, I so keep pushing, and crowding, and jamming myself on all the time …?" He goes on to say, "By heaven, man, we are turned round and round in this world, like yonder windlass, and Fate is the handspike." Ahab looks up, but Starbuck has walked away in despair at Ahab's fatalism. Ahab crosses the deck and, peering into the water, is shocked to see another pair of eyes. There is Fedallah, staring down over the same rail.

Comment

"The Symphony" brings Ahab closer to salvation than he has ever been. But the movement of the chapter destroys all hope. The title is very significant; if we take the word "symphony" in the simple poetic sense of "harmony," it may be said that there are four "symphonic levels" in the chapter:

1. The symphony (expressed in **metaphors** of maleness and femaleness) of sea and air to make a beautiful day.

2. The harmony of Ahab and nature, which brings a tear to Ahab's eye for the only time that we know of.

3. The harmony between Ahab and Starbuck, when it appears that their concord may end the search for Moby Dick.

4. The ugly harmony at the end, when Ahab stares into the water and sees the eyes of Fedallah, the man who will lead him to his fate, and share it with him. This last "harmony" is, of course, really discord; the symphony ends on a grotesque note.

CHAPTER CXXXIII: THE CHASE-FIRST DAY

On the night of the "symphony" Ahab smells the unmistakable odor of a whale, and gives a slight change of course in the direction from which the smell seems to come. At daybreak the mast-heads are manned, and Ahab himself is the first to see the whale-Moby Dick. The boats are put over, and the men paddle silently after the great whale, which seems to be swimming with a "gentle joyousness" and "a mighty mildness of repose in swiftness." The boats are almost upon Moby Dick, when suddenly he sounds. "An hour," says Ahab, but immediately the sea birds begin to circle near Ahab's boat (a sign that a whale is near), and, peering into the depths, Ahab sees the immense, open jaw of the whale rising toward him. The men whirl the boat around, but, as if in anticipation of the maneuver, Moby Dick twists under the water, and grips the boat gently in the long scroll of his jaw. He toys with the boat, squeezing the springy gunwales in and out: then he crunches the boat in half, dumping the crew into the sea. As Moby Dick swims off, Ahab and his crew are picked up by Stubb's boat, and all return to the Pequod to follow the whale.

Comment

Even though Ahab has been defeated ignominiously, his rage against the whale is impressive as he tries to pry Moby Dick's jaws off the boat with only his hands. Note the subtle use of description in this chapter: the sea, Moby Dick as he swims, Fedallah's absolute stillness as he faces death in the whale's jaws, the "still-life" of the boat as Moby Dick munches it before snapping it in half. The sense of quiet, in spite of violence, in this chapter contrasts with the sense of noisy, helter-skelter activity in the next.

CHAPTER CXXXIV: THE CHASE-SECOND DAY

At dawn the mast-heads are manned again, and the Pequod presses on after the White Whale. The crew, excited by the chase, are all welded into a unit, guided only by Ahab's purpose. The watch mistakenly calls that he has seen Moby Dick early in the morning, but later, less than a mile ahead, the whale breaches-rockets straight up out of the depths at top speed, and shoots full length out of the water. (We are told ominously, "in some cases, this breaching is his act of defiance.")

Again the boats are lowered, and again Ahab tells Starbuck to stay with the ship. This time, however, Moby Dick charges the boats instead of waiting to be attacked; he dashes among them with jaws open and tail lashing furiously. By skillful maneuvering the boats avoid him, and all three dart harpoons into his sides. As the whale thrashes about in the sea, the lines become entangled and snarled all over his body. Although Ahab daringly cuts some of the lines with his knife, the tangle drags together the boats of Stubb and Flask, smashing them to bits. Moby Dick dips beneath the surface and rises again, capsizing Ahab's boat, then floats silently, feeling with his fins for objects in the water. Whenever he feels anything, he smashes down his monstrous tail. Then he swims placidly away as the Pequod sails up to pick up the boat crews.

When Ahab is once more on deck, two facts are discovered: his ivory leg has again been broken, and Fedallah is missing (the first part of his prophecy to Ahab has been fulfilled). Undaunted, Ahab gives orders to continue on the whale's track, although Starbuck protests that this is "worse than devil's madness." Ahab's answer to Starbuck is the same one he has given before: "This whole act's immutably decreed. ... I am the Fate's lieutenant; I act under orders." As the men spring to their duty, Ahab admits to himself that he too is beginning to fear the omens all around him.

CHAPTER CXXXV: THE CHASE-THIRD DAY

The third morning is fair again, and the Pequod hastens onward. By noontime, however, there is still no sign of the whale, and

Ahab concludes that the ship has sailed past Moby Dick during the night ("He's chasing me now; not I him - that's bad"). The ship is turned about, and Ahab again has Starbuck hoist him up to the mast-head, where he sights Moby Dick after perhaps one hour's watch. Again three boats are lowered; again Starbuck remains with the ship. This time, however, numbers of sharks follow Ahab's whaleboat.

In the distance the whale dives, but the boats move onward slowly, hoping to be near him when he surfaces. Suddenly the sea around them swells, and Moby Dick races to the surface, his giant brow thirty feet in the air. Surging among the boats, he does enough minor damage to Stubb's and Flask's boats that they must go back to the ship for repairs; then the whale starts to swim away. But as he turns he exposes one of his flanks to Ahab. There on the whale's side, entangled in the snarled harpoon line, is the torn body of the Parsee. (This horrible sight fulfills the second part of the Parsee's prophecy in Chapter CXVII, that Ahab would see a "hearse" - the whale carrying the body - not made by human hands.) Nonetheless Ahab races after the whale, and darts a harpoon into him. In beginning his run, Moby Dick spills one oarsman completely out of the boat; this man is left floating astern. The whale snaps the line, and turns upon his pursuers - but instead of attacking Ahab, he charges the ship, which he sees bearing down on the scene. Ahab tries desperately to head him off, but he cannot; Moby Dick's immense forehead staves in the Pequod's starboard bow, and the ship rapidly fills with water. Ahab, enraged, darts another harpoon into Moby Dick, but as he stoops to clear a snarl in the line, it loops around his neck and snaps him out of the boat in an instant. He is gone forever. As the Pequod sinks, the great whirlpool it creates sucks everything with it, including Ahab's lone boat. As it sinks out of sight, Tashtego's arm pins a sky-hawk against the top of the mainmast. The ship, "like Satan, would not sink to hell until she had carried a part of the living heaven with her." The whirlpool settles, and "the great white shroud of the sea rolled on as it rolled five thousand years ago."

Comment

In depicting the end of Ahab's quest, Melville uses the same type of colossal effects which he employed in "The Candles" (Chapter CXIX), with even greater effect. The silent immensity of the sea, unchanged by five thousand years, bespeaks the impossibility of man's attempt to force his will upon the universe.

EPILOGUE

One last time we hear the solemn, reflective tones of Ishmael. He was, he tells us, the oarsman who was dumped out of Ahab's boat. Far from the scene, he saw Moby Dick destroy the ship, but was not pulled under by the revolving wheel of the Pequod's vortex because of his distance from the disaster. As he floated, the coffin-lifebuoy (symbol of life and death) "shot lengthwise from the sea" (as did, ironically, Moby Dick, also a symbol of both vibrant life and horrible death). For a day and a night he floated on the coffin in a calm sea, marvelously preserved from the sharks, Then he was picked up by the ship Rachel, "that in her retracing search after her missing children, only found another orphan."

Comment

Ishmael, the orphan, outcast, and wanderer, went to sea to discover something of the meaning and mystery of life. He found himself, instead, alone in the middle of the vast pitiless ocean. Is this the secret of life? Perhaps not. Perhaps he is hinting that the brotherly love of Queequeg-symbolized in the coffin that saved his life - and the parental love represented by the Rachel make sense of a life that seems a meaningless, unfriendly ocean.

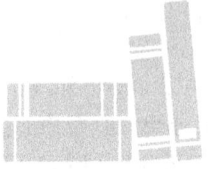

MOBY DICK

CHARACTER ANALYSES

AHAB

Ahab is basically a noble and intelligent man whose balance has been disturbed by the blind and purposeless fury of the whale that eventually destroys him. He is a man capable of love, but love by no means predominates in him. He shows "his humanities" a few times, notably at the end of the book: when he pities Pip and takes him under his care; when, with Starbuck, he reflects upon his past life; when he orders Starbuck to stay with the ship rather than risk his life battling Moby Dick. But his pride dominates his love. For example, he tells Pip that he will murder him rather than be swayed by Pip's pleading that he abandon his quest for vengeance. Several times he is brutally cutting to Starbuck; he also threatens once to murder him. He absolutely cannot comprehend the patience of the longsuffering blacksmith, asking him, "How canst thou endure without going mad?" (Even Pip's madness, though caused by what Ahab would consider weakness, makes more sense to him than the blacksmith's acceptance of the cruelties of life.)

His pride (in a sense, a prideful intelligence) also shows in his caustic treatment of his intellectual inferiors: he is contemptuous of the stupid carpenter, and he roars, "Down, dog, and kennel!" at Stubb early in the novel. He tends to despise those who do not see the universe as he sees it. But perhaps the center of his pride lies in the fact that he is not content merely to "see" more than other men (whether what he "sees" exists or not), but wishes to exert his power over what he sees. He seems to want to make the world over; he seeks to destroy the whale to prove that man is greater than the power that hides behind the "pasteboard masks" of physical reality. His pride, though it comes from a terrible sense of hurt with which we can sympathize, is essentially blasphemous. His desire for revenge is directed at God, or whatever Ahab considers to be God, rather than merely at the whale, and this urge to be avenged is all the more shocking because directed at such a vague object. Whatever power controls the universe, Ahab wants to attack it as he feels he has been attacked. The vastness of his objective sets Ahab apart from most tragic figures, as does the fact that, even with his dying breath, he refuses to repent for his actions.

ISHMAEL

Ishmael is perhaps the most important character, ultimately, in the novel. He is the filter through which all is told to us; his is the mind which orders and evaluates the experiences of the book. He contrasts with Ahab in that his is an almost purely reflective intelligence, whereas Ahab's mind drives always toward action. Ishmael wishes to understand the meaning of the world, and is appalled by the terrifying vacancy of life's mysteries (recall his concentration on the horrors of whiteness and of the bottomless, limpid blue sea). But Ahab wants to drive beyond this understanding, and remake the world to his own specifications. Ishmael avoids the "woe that is madness," but Ahab is entrapped in that woe. Ishmael is the wiser.

Ishmael is by no means merely a detached observer, however; he does actively involve himself in life. As he tells us in the first chapter, he is interested in adventure, and believes in being "on friendly terms with all the inmates of the place one lodges in." Furthermore, he becomes fast friends with a man whose background and character are radically different from his own. He is a person whose interests and sympathies are virtually limitless.

Two other fundamental qualities of Ishmael should be kept in mind: he is an unusually perceptive person; and (despite a profoundly serious nature) he is gifted with a fine sense of humor. His perceptiveness not only enables him to present *Moby Dick* to us; it is a necessary aspect of Melville's technique. (Imagine what *Moby Dick* would be like if Ishmael were a stupid person.) His humor enables him to preserve his own balance while keeping the novel from becoming an unmitigated record of catastrophes.

STARBUCK

The names of the mates are transparently significant. "Starbuck" suggests one who "bucks the stars" - fights the destiny which Ahab is pridefully shaping for the crew. He is an idealist, but a trusting and hopeful one; he does not take action. Perhaps he hasn't enough "shark" in him, to use one of *Moby Dick*'s oft-repeated metaphors.

Melville's decision to make the Pequod's first mate a man like Starbuck is both an effective and a natural one: it is the second in command whose duty it would be (especially from the viewpoint of the ship's owners) to contradict Ahab as Starbuck does. It is only to Starbuck that Melville gives both the imagination and intelligence to realize the physical and moral dangers of Ahab's quest, and the authority to do something about the situation in an emergency. To have given such qualities to the other two mates would be purposeless. And yet Starbuck is also a superstitious and, in some ways, indecisive person. The result is a blend of authority and righteousness with uncertainty and procrastination that is excruciating for both Starbuck and the reader.

STUBB

Stubb, the jolly man, is not completely stupid, but he wants to enjoy life as much as he can. He is aware of the folly of Ahab's aim, but he cannot conceive of the possibility of man's guiding and shaping his own density. (Remember that he is a professed fatalist.) He accepts life as it is without seriously questioning it-unlike Ishmael, Ahab, or Starbuck. His natural joviality leads him to optimistic distortions of the truth, as when, in Chapter CXXI, he misinterprets the meaning of Ahab's challenge to nature in Chapter CXX. Recall, however, that despite that jovial optimism, it is Stubb who abandons Pip to the sea. He might possibly reflect Melville's concept of what most men are like- for notice that, although he is not qualitatively as important as Starbuck, he says and does far more.

FLASK

Flask, aptly named "Kingpost," is a materialistic blockhead who can only see a job to be done; he never questions, never imagines, never thinks. When Stubb warns him that Ahab has some dangerous scheme in mind for the Pequod, Flask is simply skeptical. When Stubb tells him of the symbolic dream he has had (in Chapter XXX), Flask merely replies, "I don't know; it seems sort of foolish to me." Flask cruelly stabs a maimed old whale in a cancerous growth on its side; he can picture only a vast quantity of cigars when contemplating the doubloon which Ahab has nailed to the mast. Melville belittles him indirectly by mentioning how insignificant he looks in the whaleboat, when standing on the giant Daggoo's shoulders.

THE HARPOONERS

As a group, the three savages seem to sum up the good and bad points of raw human nature. They seem morally neutral; they are unmoved by storm, sea, or other terrors of nature; they accept the quest for Moby Dick, and thereafter are impassive. But they donate blood for Ahab's terrible harpoon, and they drink the blasphemous toast from the harpoon heads. Ironically, it is one of these-Queequeg, "George Washington cannibalistically developed" - who is the book's outstanding symbol of human love and brotherhood.

QUEEQUEG

Queequeg is outgoing; he befriends the greenhorn Ishmael and goes to sea with him. He is also loyal to his beliefs and his friendships, as is demonstrated several times. (For instance, he fulfills the rigorous demands of his ramadan unflinchingly. He risks his life to save Tashtego. Far more important is his symbolic "loyalty" at the end of the novel, when his coffin saves Ishmael's life.)

THE MANXMAN

(So called because he comes from the Isle of Man.) Like most of the minor characters, the Manxman is developed only slightly. His function is mainly to interpret several of the omens encountered by the Pequod, and to utter ominous sentiments of his own. He is thus a kind of prophet figure, differing from the other "prophets" of the book (Elijah, the old squaw Tistig, Gabriel of the Jeroboam, and others) in that he reappears throughout the novel.

PIP

Little Pip represents the extreme opposite of Ahab. Like Ahab, he has been dealt a smashing blow by life, but he has not been capable of surviving it. His passiveness contrasts with Ahab's titanic protests; his madness is acquiescence, Ahab's is violent protest. But Pip's essence is love; Ahab, capable, perhaps, of great love, smothers his humanity with hateful pride.

FEDALLAH

Fedallah presents one of the most sharply debated problems in *Moby Dick*. Is he simply a Parsee? Is he "simply" the Devil? Is he a symbol for pure evil, or the principle of evil disembodied from its agent (Ahab)? Is he the consciousness of sin? Note that we can ask these questions meaningfully only because Melville knew enough not to overexpose Fedallah-he is a muted, shadowy figure throughout the book.

THE CARPENTER

The carpenter serves chiefly as a foil to Ahab, to show the difference between the reactions of an intelligent and supersensitive man, and those of an unimaginative moron, to the inexplicable mysteries and cruelties of life.

THE BLACKSMITH

Again we have a character who is deliberately contrasted with Ahab. Unlike the carpenter, the blacksmith is not a stupid person: he is a man who has accepted-without being destroyed by-his fate. The blacksmith, the carpenter, and Pip should be compared in terms of their relationship to Ahab's character.

BOOMER AND BUNGER

These two officers or the ship Samuel Enderby likewise exist mainly to contrast with Ahab. Indeed, all the ships' commanders in the novel should be examined in the light of Ahab's character, for, using Ahab as the touchstone, we can see that these commanders represent a wide range of possible reactions to the limits which reality (in the form of Moby Dick's destructive power) imposes upon man. Boomer and Bunger are especially interesting, however, because they are the first to give Ahab direct information regarding Moby Dick, and because they have genuine personalities of their own.

MOBY DICK

Moby Dick is obviously intended by Melville to be, on the merely physical level, a "whale among whales," one whose size, strength, coloration, and seeming intelligence and malignity put him in a class by himself. Beyond the physical level, however, Moby Dick may be seen to have various significations (many of which derive force directly from his physical characteristics).

To Ahab he is either an evil creature in himself or the agent of an evil force that controls the universe, or perhaps both. (Certainly he is physical evil, in the sense that any physical misfortune is spoken of as "physical evil." Whatever his moral significance, if any, Moby Dick is the cause of Ahab's losing his leg.) In another sense, the reader can objectively see the White Whale as a representation of the physical limits which life imposes upon man: in other words, man cannot do whatever he wants; some things are simply beyond his power. If we reject Ahab's view of the whale, we may go to the opposite extreme: it is not the whale, but Ahab who is evil; the whale is good. From this viewpoint, of course, Moby Dick can be considered (and has been considered by some critics) to be God, or a natural agency of God, or an instrument of God's vengeance upon evil man. Notice that none of these interpretations of Moby Dick's significance attempts to minimize the fact that he is, first of all, not a symbol but a whale, except that which rather hastily assumes that Moby Dick is some kind of direct symbol for God.

To Ishmael, Moby Dick seems to mean other things. He is an astonishing force, an immense power. What appears to be uppermost in Ishmael's reaction to him is a sense of mystery: here is a phenomenon of existence that defies rational explanation. For Ishmael the White Whale perhaps represents the tremendous organic vitality of the universe, an impersonal life-force which surges onward irresistibly, impervious to the desires or wills of men. He is thus to be regarded with respect (perhaps even with fear), but hardly in anger. He also becomes, from this viewpoint, a source of intense speculation, an object of profound curiosity.

Beyond these symbolic levels, Moby Dick presents still other meanings (usually vigorously debated) to modern psychological criticism. Moby Dick is to some Freudians a great phallic symbol; his immense vitality becomes, not simply an obvious symbol of the vitality of the universe, but a projection of a subconscious awareness of the principle of life. To other critics he is the male principle, or a projection of the Father (especially since he "punishes" Ahab), or even, in a sense, a symbol of the Mother (the whale's head and belly are likened to both a womb and a tomb by some). He is our "universal parents" in this view. That the psychological approach has its limitations as well as its fascination should be obvious from this sketch.

Ultimately it is best to remember that Moby Dick is a whale-a gigantic beast-first, and a symbol next. The impact of the whale's symbolic meanings derive largely from Ishmael-Melville's careful examination of the whale's organism; it will not do to ignore the elemental physical immediacy of the encounter with the whale.

MOBY DICK

CRITICAL COMMENTARY

Moby Dick was published in London in mid-October, 1851, under the title *The Whale*; on November 14, it was published as *Moby-Dick, or the Whale* in New York. Several reviews were printed in England in late October and early November. The attitude of the critics was varied, but the general tone of the reviews was negative. In particular, two very influential periodicals, the *Athenaeum* and *the Spectator*, treated the book harshly. Even the favorable reviews tended to question the book's form or style, and many were disturbed by Melville's attitude toward organized religion.

In November the first American reviews of *Moby Dick* were printed. Generally they were quite favorable (though perhaps partly because Melville's earliest works, *Typee* and *Omoo*, had been very popular). But as time passed, further reviews of the book became less and less favorable; in a few years the book was all but forgotten. When Melville died in 1891, he was remembered (if at all) not for *Moby Dick*, but for *Typee* and *Omoo*.

The story of the revival of Melville's reputation is one of the most interesting in the history of American literature. It may be said to begin in 1921 with a biography by Raymond Weaver, called *Herman Melville, Mariner and Mystic*. Weaver was enthusiastically pro-Melville. He called *Moby Dick* "indisputably the greatest whaling novel." In 1929 came another key book, Lewis Mumford's Herman Melville. Mumford worked not so much on the facts of Melville's life as on "reconstructing" Melville's mind. His book is a daring and speculative one, which uses Melville's fiction, to a certain extent, as autobiographical documents (a highly questionable method). Nonetheless the study is a stimulating one; Mumford's attempt to integrate Melville's life and his works was extremely important in inspiring further studies. Investigations of various kinds-some speculative, some of a most rigidly factual nature-followed for the next ten years. In 1939, Charles R. Anderson published an extremely important study of *Melville in the South Seas*, which provides a counterbalance to speculations like Mumford's. It is an extremely close study of factual data connected with Melville during the three years he was in the Pacific. Further, it suggests very strongly a different picture of Melville's mind from that of the earlier works: it shows that Melville shaped and transformed factual material rather than simply "inventing" things.

From the mid-1940s to the mid-1950s there was an especially large quantity of writing on Melville. W. E. Sedgwick, in *Herman Melville: The Tragedy of Mind* (1945), finds a "trinity" in *Moby Dick*: Ahab, Man, comes into conflict with Moby Dick the whale, "the immense mystery of creation." The third element of this trinity is the ocean, which represents "truth." In 1949 appeared Richard Chase's *Herman Melville: A Critical Study*, a book with a very strong psychological and symbolical bias. Chase felt that the most important **theme** of Melville's work before *Moby Dick* was that of the young man's awakening, or introduction to experience (a common **theme** in romantic literature). Chase's book is dangerous, in some ways, because it asserts a good deal which it makes no attempt to prove. One year later, Newton Arvin published a short, highly readable biography called simply *Herman Melville*. The best chapter in the book is called "The Whale." Among other things, Arvin opines that the form of *Moby Dick* is closer to heroic poetry and the **epic** than to any other literary type. He discusses the structure, symbolism, and language of the book effectively. But many readers and critics find his treatment of Moby Dick as a symbol of "the father" an objectionable one. Arvin stresses the sexual innuendoes which are found frequently in the novel, as does Leslie Fiedler in a more recent work, *Love and Death in the American Novel* (1960). The relationship of Ishmael and Queequeg, for instance, and the suggestive descriptions of the whale, are anatomized at length by these two writers and by others who have found the Freudian approach to Melville fruitful.

In a sense, the next biographical study counteracts many of the views of both Chase and Arvin. Leon Howard, in *Herman Melville* (1950), rejects the critical concept which assumes that the subconscious mind is of primary importance in writing: he says, "in dealing with Melville's books I have concerned myself primarily with the observable evidence of their growth." In 1951, a fresh look at Melville was provided by an Englishman, Ronald Mason, in a book called *The Spirit Above the Dust: A Study of Herman Melville*. Mason admits that there are some "loose ends" in "a book which by its very compendiousness could hardly hope to avoid them," but feels that *Moby Dick* is nevertheless a great work; the transformation of "symbolic images into a creative myth, embodying a significant reflection of the profoundest human pre-occupations, was Melville's achievement in *Moby Dick*." For Mason, *Moby Dick* embodies Melville's own philosophic despair: "the finest novel America has yet given to the world, it proclaims unmistakably Melville's spiritual desolation."

Criticism and commentary on Melville and *Moby Dick* has continued to mount in the last decade, especially in articles and essays. A vast range of attitudes toward the book has been expressed: it has been read as myth, poem, political allegory, psychological document, and in various other ways. A possible explanation for the variety of viewpoints is to be found in John Parke's essay, "Seven Moby-Dick's" (see the annotated bibliography). Parke finds seven levels of meaning in *Moby Dick*. It is: an adventure saga; an adventure with a vague spiritual tone; an "emblem-story of man and nature"; a burning symbolic representation of "a profound conflict in the soul of man"; an allegory of man's attack upon nature (and thus, in a sense, upon himself); a paradoxical presentation of a man whose actions we condemn, yet regard as a sort of hero (involving us in theological questions about the nature of the universe); and last, a study of a man in revolt against evil and chaos in the universe. If we can accept Parke's analysis, or one similar to it, we can readily understand why there are so many and such conflicting ideas regarding *Moby Dick*. Which of these levels will a critic stress, and why?

Interest in Melville's mind and inner attitudes has bulked large in Melville criticism of the past decade or so. One of the most famous psychological treatments of *Moby Dick* is Henry Murray's "In Nomine Diaboli"; Murray says that *"Moby-Dick* may be taken as a comment on the strategic crisis of Melville's allegorical life." It reveals various internal conflicts in Melville's makeup, which Melville is attempting to resolve artistically through *Moby Dick*. Murray feels that Melville did not solve his problems through this novel, but only many years later, as his death approached. (The interesting, but also the dangerous aspects for psychological criticism should be clear from this hint of the contents of Mr. Murray's essay. To what extent, and on what level, are we to look for the influence of a man's life history upon his writings?)

Perhaps this brief discussion of *Moby Dick* criticism should close with an example of another approach to the book which has been very popular in recent years, that of the "myth critic." In "*Moby Dick*: The Myth of Democratic Expectancy," Harry Slochower argues that *Moby Dick* embodies a vision of American character on the borderline "between individualism and coordination, between freedom and equality." In effect, it poses the question, "What is the American?" Ahab, in Slochower's view, succeeds in imposing his personal will upon the crew (who otherwise have no interest in *Moby Dick*) because they have no collective identity - no common ideals. *Moby Dick* differs from most myths in that it does not rehabilitate or redeem its hero, but it has at least the basic elements of the traditional pattern of myths. Slochower summarizes the mythic importance of *Moby Dick* in these terms; "Melville's *Moby Dick* is the first major American literary myth sounding the central motifs of creation and quest. Its distinctive American quality lies in its uncertain attitude toward creation."

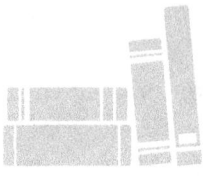

MOBY DICK

ESSAY QUESTIONS AND ANSWERS

Question: *Moby Dick* is often considered an **epic**. In what ways does the work fit the category of epic?

Answer: An **epic** is a long narrative which presents characters of high position in a series of adventures of high significance. Usually the **epic** is unified around a central figure of heroic stature, and generally it deals with actions of great importance to a nation or people. *Moby Dick* is clearly a long tale of adventures which are profoundly meaningful, for they make us feel deeply the dangers of pride and hatred, and they bring forth much of the inexplicable mystery of life. Ahab is a character of gigantic proportions, even though we may shudder at him even as we admire (and perhaps pity) him. Symbolically, the actions are important on a national level, for the story can be read as an allegory of the risks involved in trying to subjugate nature to the will of man-a danger quite obvious to Americans in a century in which the annihilation of humanity has become a possibility.

Besides these general considerations, however, there are specific ways in which *Moby Dick* seems epical: 1. It uses a long journey (journeys, especially sea voyages, are standard in epics);

2. It uses elevated language frequently, especially at moments of high passion; 3. There are a series of battles, which remind one of the single combats of ancient epics; 4. Omens and, apparently, God's intervention function significantly in the novel as in the **epic**; 5. The extensive description of the implements of whaling and the ways of a whaler's life parallel the description of arms and warriors in early epics; 6. A sense of a pervasive influence of fate in life reminds us of some epics. Other parallels can easily be drawn, although we may be tempted into some comparisons that are strained (for instance, do the immersions in water, especially Tashtego's in the whale's head, parallel the **epic** journey to the underworld?").

Question: What kind of narrative technique does Melville use?

Answer: Actually, Melville employs not one technique, but several. Most important, of course, is Ishmael, the first-person narrator of the book. But even this primary narrative device is complex; Ishmael seems to be more than one person-or at least more than one viewpoint. There is the older, wiser Ishmael who tells the story, and the younger Ishmael who experiences its events. There is also the Ishmael who is more or less involved in, or observing, the action, and then there is the philosophic Ishmael who examines all this experience and tries to understand its meaning in the ultimate scheme of things.

We see several other techniques used: 1. The dramatic method, as in Chapters XXXVI and XL, which even use stage directions; 2. The dramatic monologue, in Chapters XXXVII through XXXIX (XXXVII can even be called an interior or psychological monologue); 3. The catalogue, as in "Cetology" (Chapter XXXII); 4. The device of the story-within-a-story ("The Town-Ho's Story," Chapter LIV); 5. The "omniscient author" technique-several times we get information which Ishmael could not possibly give us, and at other times the tone of the narrative is definitely not Ishmael's. Further variation in the novel is achieved by occasional flashbacks and reminiscences.

Question: How does Melville's method of characterization help him to develop his themes?

Answer: Melville's characters, with the possible exception of Ahab, are not developed from within, but in terms of their relationship to others or to external forces. Ahab is a character with many facets, but the others seem to be one-sided, with their function that of contrasting with each other or with some aspect of Ahab. Thus Starbuck becomes an embodiment of the well-meaning but indecisive man of faith, contrasting with Ahab's driving hate and skepticism. Stubb's refusal to think and his happy-go-lucky temperament contrast with Ahab's and Starbuck's intellectual seriousness, and Flask's materialistic stupidity contrast with all the others. Just as important, these four characters all react very differently to Moby Dick, to nature, and to life in general-keeping us aware that the novel is not only about Ahab, but about the ways men confront the world they live in as well.

The other characters function in much the same manner. Queequeg is marvelously impressive - we admire his skill, his bravery, and his selflessness - but we never really come to know him as a person. He is there for what he does and what he is, not for who he is. Tashtego and Daggoo are merely savages - they represent an attitude toward life, and are far less complete as people than Queequeg. The carpenter and blacksmith are likewise merely types, with no real life of their own. The Manxman mouths important oracular sayings, but has no personality. Fedallah is evil, but he is simply an ugly presence, not a human being. Pip, of course, is a fuller character.

To say all this is not to attack Melville's characterization-far from it. It is simply to point out that he is interested in reflecting various attitudes toward life, and does this - very successfully - through his characters. He has no desire to introduce us to each character in the fullness of his humanity, but rather, we might say, to the narrowness of his humanity. Ironically, he richest, ripest person in the whole novel is hardly a "character" at all - for it is Ishmael whom we come to know best of all, and who gives us most of himself.

Question: How can the inclusion of so much factual detail about whales and whaling be justified?

Answer: The whaling material has often erroneously been considered mere journalism, or even mere padding. Even as journalism or history, the whaling details are of value, for they publicize the history of a once-major industry which would otherwise be hidden in specialized books on whaling. But there are far more important artistic justifications. First, the whaling data give the book a certain leisurely pace; it might otherwise have raced to, rather than built up to, its furious conclusion. Second, the cetology provides a sort of "ballast" for the book-keeps it thoroughly in touch with actuality when Ishmael-Melville's desire to philosophize and speculate might otherwise have made the book too abstract and merely "talky." Most important, the material on whales and whaling provides the raw material out of which Ishmael can develop the meaning of Ahab's quest and of his own experience. The whale is his (and Melville's) **metaphor** for the whole of experience: it is alive and changing, complex and impossible to explain, mysterious and beautiful, and powerful and terrifying. All these aspects are underscored as, from time to time, Ishmael ponders one or another part or characteristic of the whale. The constant preoccupation of Ishmael (and thus the entire novel) with the whale keeps us constantly immersed in the metaphorical "raw material" of Melville's view of the world.

Question: What is the significance or function of the Pequod's encounters with other ships?

Answer: First we must recognize that the "gams" are realistic parts of an actual whaling voyage, and that on the reportorial level Melville is again doing a fascinating job of writing. Second, the other ships are the "society" of the world of the Pequod, and the gams stress the thoroughly unsocial nature of the ship's voyage under Captain Ahab. We might extend this conception somewhat and say that, because of Ahab's obsession, the Pequod is not merely unsociable but anti-social in the literal sense. (Not simply desirous of avoiding "company," but actually of attacking the very foundation and values upon which society is built. The quest is, after all, a fanatical violation on Ahab's part of both the purpose of whaling and of respect for other human beings.) A third function of these meetings is that they serve as warnings, although unheeded, of the Pequod's fate if it continues the quest. From the first encounter with the Goney (Albatross), through the mad prophecies of Gabriel, to the desolate burials at sea in the case of the Rachel and the Delight, Ahab is being warned time and again that Moby Dick embodies a power that is simply too great for man to conquer. But in every case he ignores the omens, even when, toward the end of the novel, he increasingly believes that they are omens and not merely accidents. The heightening ominousness of the gams builds tension, and the increasing horror of Moby Dick's destructiveness makes it appear all the more likely that the outcome will be catastrophic.

Question: What is the function of the repeated **imagery** in *Moby Dick*?

Answer: So many images are repeated so as to fall into recognizable patterns that only one such image can be discussed at all thoroughly in a brief answer. One that might be mentioned is that having to do with being trapped by the whale in one way or another. The Jonah motif, which runs throughout the novel, is one aspect of this system of entrapment images (though it might well be considered all by itself). Various men are "swallowed" by the whale - Jonah in Mapple's sermon, Tashtego when he falls into the whale's head-or are maimed by the whale's jaws, such as Ahab himself, Radney of the Town-Ho, and Macey of the Jeroboam. This is only the beginning, however: as a stone cast into the water spreads concentric ripples, the basic image spreads meanings on several levels. Who else is "swallowed" by the whale? Why, says Ishmael (thinking of Tashtego) those who "have likewise fallen into Plato's honey head, and sweetly perished there." Who else has gone into the whale's jaws? Anyone who has walked into the bar at the Spouter-Inn, with its archway of a whale's jawbone, or anyone who signs on the Pequod, that "cannibal of a craft," with its bulwarks of jawbone with the teeth still intact, or anyone who has pulled headlong into the jaws of destruction when attacking a whale. In fact, when Ishmael first signs up for the whaling voyage, Captain Peleg asks him, "art thou the man to pitch a harpoon down a live whale's throat, and then jump after it?"

One need not be swallowed by the whale to be trapped by it, however. Many a whaleboat is caught and pulled under by its own harpoon rope. Captain Boomer is caught and torn by his second harpoon, attached to the line he has managed to get fast to Moby Dick. Pip is once caught in a whale line. Fedallah is entangled in the lines wrapped around Moby Dick. Ahab is snapped from his boat forever when the line catches him about the neck. Small wonder that Ishmael states, in Chapter LX, "All men live enveloped in whale-lines"! Both on the level of action and on that of Ishmael's reflections, the images of entrapment and destruction by the whale are constantly before us.

What is the purpose of this kind of repetition? For one thing, it grinds out what seems to be an inexorable fatality in *Moby Dick*. The reader is forewarned, and Ahab is forewarned, by constant recurrence of the same ominous motif. As Ahab will do nothing to break the pattern, the reader becomes excruciatingly aware of the fate which seems to be in store for Ahab. Thus the repetition creates both a premonition of the **catastrophe** and a tone, endlessly oppressive and tense. Repetition also provides Melville with a mode of exposing different reactions to the dangers of whaling and to Moby Dick particularly. Last, but absolutely not least important, these repeated images overlap with other sets of images in the novel and constantly lead to new and richer aspects of *Moby Dick's* themes. The teeth of the whale remind us of the tearing teeth of the sharks, and "universal cannibalism." The rope which links the whaleman to his prey, and which destroys Fedallah and Ahab, also links Ishmael to Queequeg in the bond of brotherhood, and connects the men in the whaleboat in a joint effort. The power which causes Jonah - and the godfearing Captain Boomer - to thank God for deliverance, drives Ahab to hate. On and on these images go, as complex and interwoven, one might say, as the whale lines entangled on Moby Dick's body.

BIBLIOGRAPHY AND GUIDE TO FURTHER RESEARCH

There are many books and hundreds of articles on Melville and *Moby Dick*. Probably the two best introductory works for the newcomer to Melville are James G. Miller's *A Reader's Guide to Herman Melville* (1962, paperback), and Willard Thorp's "Introduction" to *Herman Melville: Representative Selections* (1938), still excellent though dated in some ways. The following list of biographical and critical studies is highly selective. The starred items are available in paperback editions. Additional bibliography can be found in the following sources, among others:

1. *Eight American Authors*, edited by Floyd Stoval (1956). This book discusses the contents of the works it lists, and is extremely helpful as a general orientation for criticism of Melville.*

2. *Modern Fiction Studies*, Vol. VIII, no. iii (a "Herman Melville Special Number"). This 1962 issue has excellent listings of criticism.

Biography (arranged chronologically)

Mumford. Lewis, *Herman Melville* (1929). Develops a picture of Melville as a daring imaginative giant.

Arvin, Newton, *Herman Melville* (1950). Not the best factual biography, but perhaps the most readable. Freudian bias, stresses the influence on Melville of the shock caused by the death of his father.*

Howard, Leon, *Herman Melville: A Biography* (1951). The most trustworthy biography for facts, especially good if read with the following work.*

Leyda, Jay, *The Melville Log* (1951). A compendium of data about Melville, arranged chronologically (in two volumes). Leyda lets the reader make his own judgments about what the facts mean for Melville's life.

BOOK-LENGTH STUDIES OF MELVILLE OR MOBY DICK

A few of these works are virtually biographies. All of them deal with *Moby Dick* to some extent.

Anderson, Charles R., *Melville in the South Seas* (1939). Covers the years 1841 to 1844; much biographical data.

Bowen, Merlin, *The Long Encounter: Self and Experience in the Writings of Herman Melville* (1960). Develops the interesting idea that Melville's characters fall into three basic types: those who fight fate, those who give in, and those who preserve "armed neutrality." Helpful short chapter introduction.

Braswell, William, *Melville's Religious Thought* (1943). Now somewhat dated, but still the most complete introduction to this aspect of Melville.

Chase, Richard, *Herman Melville: A Critical Study* (1949). A controversial, but stimulating book which stresses mythic and psychological aspects of Melville's fiction. Tries to see Melville both as artist and in relation to cultural problems.

Mason, Ronald, *The Spirit Above the Dust, a Study of Herman Melville* (1951). Gives a fresh view in many ways, because the author is English. Central **theme** is that Melville concentrates on innocence in his early works, the loss of innocence later, and the triumph of innocence in Billy Budd, Melville's posthumous story.

Olsen, Charles, *Call Me Ishmael* (1947). An exciting, if opinionated, book. Especially good for the influence of Shakespeare upon *Moby Dick* and for the importance of space to Melville. Suggests that the Pequod symbolizes American industry and Ahab the American who is trying to subdue physical nature.*

Percival, M. O., *A Reading of Moby Dick* (1950). A good general guide and introduction to the novel-a running commentary.

Rosenberry, Edward, *Melville and the Comic Spirit* (1955). As the title implies, this work takes up the "other side" of Melville.

Sedgwick, W. E., *Herman Melville, the Tragedy of Mind* (1945). Concentrates on the development of Melville's "inner vision" rather than dealing with the works specifically as literature.

Thompson, Lawrance, *Melville's Quarrel with God* (1952). Argues basically that Melville hated God. An extreme book.

Vincent, Howard P., *The Trying-Out of Moby Dick* (1949). A study of what materials Melville used to write the novel. Demonstrates the importance of the whaling material to the book's theme.

Wright, Nathalia, *Melville's Use of the Bible* (1949). Traces Melville's use of the language, characters, images, and **themes** of the Bible.

COLLECTIONS OF ESSAYS ON MELVILLE AND MOBY DICK

Discussions of Moby Dick, edited by Milton Stern (1960). An outstanding collection of essays, covering several major points and representing a number of critical viewpoints. Especially helpful for the "gams."*

Melville: A Collection of Critical Essays, edited by Richard Chase (1962). Includes some of the essays printed in the Stern collection but broader in scope.*

Moby-Dick Centennial Essays, edited by Tyrus Hillway and Luther Mansfield (1953). Contains several excellent short pieces.

BOOKS WHICH DEAL IN PART WITH MELVILLE AND MOBY DICK

Chase, Richard, *The American Novel and Its Tradition* (1957). Considers *Moby Dick* as an "**epic** romance." Many stimulating comments in a few pages.*

Feidelson, Charles Jr., *Symbolism and American Literature* (1953). Sees *Moby Dick* as the high point of a symbolic movement in nineteenth-century American literature.*

Lawrence, D. H., *Studies in Classic American Literature* (1923, 1951). Devotes two very provocative chapters to Melville. Brilliant, but dangerous.*

Levin, Harry, *The Power of Blackness* (1958). Treats Poe, Hawthorne, and Melville as writers who focus on the dark side of human nature.*

Lewis, R. W. B., *The American Adam* (1957). Discusses the **theme** of the American as a "new man." One chapter on Melville.*

Matthiessen, F. O., *American Renaissance* (1940). A brilliant discussion of five authors, including Melville. Especially good for social significance of Melville; excellent discussions of language.

www.ingramcontent.com/pod-product-compliance
Lightning Source LLC
LaVergne TN
LVHW021717060526
838200LV00050B/2704